# The Alchemy
# of Caregiving

# The Alchemy of Caregiving

## Transforming Grief and Loss into Wholeness

# Karen Young

Cover design by Markos Moreno

ISBN 978-1-935914-13-6

Printed in the United States of America

To order additional copies please visit:

**www.riversanctuarypublishing.com**

RIVER SANCTUARY PUBLISHING
P.O Box 1561
Felton, CA 95018
www.riversanctuarypublishing.com
*Dedicated to the spiritual awakening of the New Earth*

## Acknowlegments

*A warm thanks to Mary Scott whose vision, clarity, and editing helped shape the story. Another warm thanks to friends whose support was ongoing: Katie Finlay-Meredith, Julia Devin, Sara Wasserman, and Dennis Harness. A final thanks to* River Sanctuary Publishing *for bringing this book to completion with grace.*

*To Jeff*

# Contents

*San Francisco, November 2007*

# INTRODUCTION

*Love says: "I am everything."*
*Wisdom says: "I am nothing."*
*Between the two, my life flows.*

—Nisargadatta Maharaj[1]

This is a story about love and loss, a journey inward and outward. It is a story about unexpectedly becoming a caregiver just as the intoxication of new love started to settle. On the surface there is stumbling, surrender, and a story of colliding beliefs. Inwardly there is a movement through reactions and the gamut of emotions as the depths of grief are navigated and the journeyer is delivered to the sweetness of gratitude for it all. It is a story of conscious living and conscious dying, a spiritual journey suffused with love. And more, there is a deepening recognition of the *Ground of Being* from which everything emerges.

I did not expect to become the caregiver of my partner so soon after we met and fell in love. Initially, Jeff lived in the San Francisco Bay area and I lived in Seattle. We were in the aliveness of the first year of new love anticipating years of curiosity, deepening love, and new adventures. We were just beginning to learn about each other's personality quirks and conditioned habits. Then Jeff was diagnosed with pancreatic cancer. Without hesitation I moved from my home—and left everything—to be with him.

In a nanosecond I became both a partner and caregiver. Caregiving was not new to me. I had worked for many years as a nurse supporting stem cell transplant patients and training and advising their families in the caretaking role. Even with that background, there were times I was at a loss to know what to do. I also had a strong spiritual foundation that provided a framework for how to approach the caregiving challenge day-to-day, moment-to-moment. The journey with Jeff illuminated where that foundation was cracked or incomplete; it relentlessly showed me where my emotional expectations and spiritual understandings seemed to diverge from the reality of life unfolding.

I discovered that the challenges of a caregiver appear insurmountable at times. I experienced sudden and difficult shifts and changes, and felt like I was forging a narrow path up a steep, rocky mountainside. Life was no longer ordinary. It was fundamentally changed by the process and progress of Jeff's terminal illness. I participated in Jeff's decision-making and worried about giving bad advice. I lived in anticipation of the loss of a great love and I grieved in anticipation of that loss. I was separated from the life I had known—home, career, friends—and I feared the loss of my very self as the pressures of being the primary caregiver closed in on me. It felt like everything was being stripped away and I clung to every little thing to forestall more change and loss.

During the days and months from the time of Jeff's diagnosis until his death, I lived with loss and grief. In her research with dying patients, Elisabeth Kübler-Ross proposed a framework to understand the process by which one comes to terms with a terminal illness or catastrophic loss. Reflecting on the challenges of my own journey, I attempted to categorize my reactions using Kübler-Ross' proposed stages of denial, anger, bargaining, depression and acceptance.[2] For me, these stages weren't little boxes into which I could neatly assign my responses. Any attempt to do so seemed to undermine the richness of genuine experience.

There is no right or wrong way to navigate loss; there are as many ways to do so as there are individuals on the planet. Eventually, loss goes deep and a transformation occurs—a shedding of skin, if you will. You can't predict what will emerge once the old skin is shed, but one thing is certain—you will be changed. There are many stories and memoirs about journeys of loss, love and change, and at times I questioned myself about the reason to write this one. But each story is unique, and I hope this account of my journey will provide insight, comfort, and validation to you as your own journey unfolds.

## ~ Chapter 1 ~

## IN THE BEGINNING

There is an oft translated quote by Lao Tzu from section sixty-four of the Tao te Ching, which states:

> *...A tree as great as a man's embrace springs from a small shoot;*
> *A terrace nine stories high begins with a pile of earth;*
> *A journey of a thousand miles starts under one's feet.*[3]

A single step began this journey: I fell in love.

It is 2007 and love happens. Love of the heart, beyond romantic love, from the deepest core. It is as if everything in life comes together to create this moment.

A Vedic astrologer and friend with whom I had once taken classes described it as a Venus cycle, the mythological Venus representing beauty and divine love. Apparently, during such a transit, Venus collects galactic love as it moves far beyond, then returns to shower this luscious nectar onto the earth—and in this case, onto my astrological chart. According to the planets and stars, this meeting was a once-in-a-lifetime cross-pollination that appears to have been predestined. My astrologer friend offered this insight several weeks after I met Jeff, suggesting that nothing could have prevented our powerful connection.

However predestined it might have been, I would never have predicted it. I was a divorced career woman, content with my single life. My job as a nurse—part of a stem cell transplant team—provided enriching challenges and gave meaning to my life. My work schedule gave me about half of each month off. I had time to enjoy meditation retreats, travel, nature, yoga, devotional chanting and friends. There was only one unfulfilled desire for which I had a deep curiosity that had been with me since childhood. Although I did not quite understand it at the time, from a young age I'd experienced a strong spiritual yearning. I wanted to know God—to know *Truth*—to know my own self deeply and intimately.

I was eight or nine years old when a curious thought crossed my mind. *In this lifetime I will experience everything and I will get it. I will know the truth of the universe.* Perhaps a bit unusual for a child, but there it was. As an adult I explored meditation, Buddhism and the writings of the Dalai Lama, Islam and Sufism while working in Kuwait; and, finally, the emerging western version of a non-dual, non-dogmatic spirituality from India called Advaita Vedanta.

Years after I was drawn to it, this approach to spirit and reality became familiar to mainstream America when Oprah popularized the non-dual teachings of

Eckhart Tolle about the journey of awakening. When Oprah and Tolle offered a webcast of non-dual course-work to a national audience, I realized this path was beginning to be discovered by many others. For me, the spiritual path had always been the most important part of life. I was happy with my spiritual journey and was not looking to be in a romantic relationship.

My sister had other ideas. She worried about me "being alone." When discussing how I spent my vacation time at silent spiritual retreats, she would often pose the question, *"How are you going to meet anybody on your retreats if you can't talk?"* She had a point, but I loved silent retreats. I wasn't looking for a partner while on retreat, or anywhere else. If it were to happen, that would be okay; if it didn't happen that was okay, too. I envisioned myself working until retirement, then aging with grace as a wise crone.

I was visiting a friend in Tucson when an opportunity arose to appease my sister. A retreat that coincided with my visit was happening in Sedona, that magical place of red rock beauty in northern Arizona. Although it wasn't silent, it was geared towards *silence.* I was somewhat ambivalent about going since I could not attend the entire retreat, but I felt something propelling me forward. I had a feeling that something much larger than myself was directing things, so I decided to "go with the flow."

Arriving at the retreat I learned that my accommodations had been changed. Initially I was to have my own room at the home of the retreat teachers. I was now to share a small room with another woman in a house filled with participants. There was an instant of disappointment. Hopefully she would not be a chatterbox—and hopefully neither of us would snore.

I love being in retreat. Being in the close quarters of a house with nine other people and sharing a bedroom was certainly different from any of my other retreat experiences. At a silent retreat, I could be perfectly happy in a room with three or four other people. No one talks; no chatty conversation needs to be made. I love silence and I love listening to the sounds of nature in that silence. To me, the silence between notes is what makes the music sing. This retreat would be something a bit different for me.

I remember my first silent retreat 25 years ago. I stayed in a little room—a Buddhist cell—with only a single bed, table and chair. Moving through the first day without talking was torture. Yet, by the end of the retreat, I loved being bathed in that silence. On the last day of that first silent retreat when everyone started talking it all sounded like mindless, egoic chatter. I realized how much of what we talk about is our own stories, egos, and conditioning. I became aware of how often very little is actually said in conversation and how little is actually heard.

So, I set out to explore the house: I wanted to find a private corner where I could meditate during the retreat. When I discovered a spacious, empty den I thought I'd found my perfect spot. However, at that moment a man walked in with a large suitcase. This was his room for the week. He introduced himself as Jeff, asked my name, and proceeded to start talking. He spoke of his life, his spiritual teachers, teachings that inspired him, and I was intrigued. Quickly he asked about teachers and teachings that I found meaningful. He seemed interested in my life and experience.

After about ten minutes of conversation about our spiritual backgrounds, Jeff asked, "Have you ever been to Bali?"

"Well, no," I replied.

He smiled, "I have enough frequent flyer miles for a trip for two around the world. Want to come?"

I could only laugh. That was the most original pick-up line I'd ever heard. Normally a line like that would send me running in the opposite direction. Surprisingly our conversation, and the connection I was already starting to feel, had me staying put. I was interested in this man and I felt something inside of me shift. My contentedly single, independent and spiritually attuned self experienced a flutter of excitement.

The heart of the spiritual path is the longing to know and live as an expression of your true Self. I didn't want a relationship to pull me away from that which was so important to me. An old Indian saying declares that once you have taken this path, *your head is in the tiger's mouth and there is no turning back.* I was committed to investigating the nature of experience, the world, the body and the mind. I had spent many years dissecting my belief in a separate *me*, and seeking experience and understanding of the spiritual state of unity that was such a compelling part of so many spiritual traditions. I wanted to know myself as that essence which is always already present and never changes.

In the minutes after meeting Jeff, all of this traversed my mind. And yet, still another thought arose and darted across my awareness. Actually, it was more than a thought, it was a *knowing*. It was quiet and barely perceptible, but very clear. *I am going to spend my life with this person.* The thought flashed by quickly—in and out. It wasn't a desire or a want; there were no bells or whistles. It was just a *knowing*. But this seed was planted in fertile soil because I had experienced similar knowings before, all of which had manifested in my life in one way or another.

The retreat was full of spiritual self-inquiry and activities. There were several satsangs daily. The literal translation of satsang is "association with Truth." It is a term that comes from the Advaita Vedanta tradition of India, and it describes a gathering when a teacher and students come together to talk, reflect, question, or meditate for the purpose of a deepening understanding of *Truth*. Teachings that emerge in satsang are pointers to what is sometimes called the vast *Ground of Being* from which everything emerges. Other traditions call this God, Spirit, Emptiness, Consciousness or Awareness. One understanding in satsang is that this primordial reality is not something that only a few saints and sages realize or become. It is what we already are in our essential nature.

In addition to the discourses, the retreat included meditation, free time and one day, a hike in silence.

After so much talking, I was happy for the chance to walk silently in nature. I found Jeff waiting for me at the trailhead for a hike that would take us through lovely woods, along a creek, and deep into a canyon. I was touched and happy that he had waited for me. When he asked if we could walk together I agreed, but reminded him that we had to be quiet. Our silence lasted about five minutes and then there was no stopping our excited talk as we began to get to know each other. That evening we continued our conversation as we sat in the living room alone, chairs facing each other, our knees touching. There was barely a brushing of knee to knee, but there was more electricity and magic in that touch than could be imagined.

"I think we should continue to get to know each other after the retreat ends," offered Jeff.

"Maybe," I said.

*Maybe?* What was I saying? This person was fabulous. Why was I hesitating? I was aware that retreat romances did not always endure once people returned to their daily lives. Was that my hesitation or was an old fear of not being good enough causing me to hold back? I hoped I was hesitating because of my desire to keep my spiritual life first in my priorities, but maybe that old uncomfortable story about inadequacy had never been resolved.

The next day there was an opportunity for free time after the morning satsang. Jeff and I headed off together with another friend for the buffet at a local Indian restaurant. During lunch, Jeff asked questions that went right to the core of the mystery of life. After our dialogue over lunch, we toured the local art galleries. Just inside the door of one gallery was a table displaying books for sale. The first book I spotted had a forward by John Denver. I commented on my love of John Denver's music. Suddenly, *Annie's Song* was being sung in my ear by Jeff. In an instant my hesitancy melted. I knew I was smitten and falling in love.

The next few days flew by. There was insightful inquiry into the *Ground of Being.* There was good food. There was also competition for Jeff's attention. Several women flirted with him and wanted to spend time with him. He was open, friendly and genuinely available to everyone.

At some point every day, Jeff managed to say the same thing to me, "I want to get to know you better. Can we continue this after the retreat is over?"

My hesitation remained, even though I was now *in love.* Perhaps I had lingering doubts about being in another relationship. Yet, something inside felt like Jeff was my soul mate. Even with that inner sense, I could only say, "Maybe, we'll see." Despite my ambivalence, deep inside I knew I was hooked and I hoped he was too.

At the end of the retreat I drove back to the Phoenix airport. Upon arriving at the airport, I learned my flight was delayed. I sat and composed some of my free-flowing poetry—writing whatever arose into my little notebook. The first line came as I sat in the airport; the rest was completed as we flew over the Grand Canyon:

*Falling in love happens every time words*
  *fall off your lips.*
*Sunset magic occurs as rich red and orange*
  *layers grace the sky's horizon over the canyon*
  *of immense beauty below.*
*Falling in love happens every time words fall*
  *off your lips.*
*What a blessing. Like being held in the most*
  *tender of lover's arms, enveloped in the lover's*
  *most tender, sweet embrace.*
*Such grace.*
*Gazing into the soul's space, there is no other.*
*There never was.*
*Seeing the love that exists in all. It's all there.*
*The questions. The answers. The silence.*
*All is held. Pure love. Rest in it.*

The words flowed through me. It felt like my heart was wide open. There was a response from Jeff a few days later. I felt like a love-struck teen upon reading it.

*Thank you so much for the poetry.*

*I am so happy to have been blessed by our meeting. At the last satsang. . .I began to cry and couldn't quite sense what it was about but it was the most delicious blend of joy and sadness I've ever felt. Gratitude was pouring out of me and the feeling that something I've held dear, painfully so, was dying. It was like my own funeral. . . Now I'm there, or better yet, "here" again thinking of you. In a way, you represent the mystery to me, the somewhat frightening unknown merging with a sense of possibility beyond my little mind's capacity to imagine. I have already fallen in love with you, lived a lifetime or two, and died before waking up to realize we haven't had our first date yet. I'm sorry if my ramblings seem that of a slightly deranged teenager but honestly that's how I feel.*

*I really only want to say that you have touched me in a way that I can't explain to you or myself, any more than my tears. Perhaps you are really inside me already and I in you. Or perhaps I have an over active imagination. Whatever...this lifetime is for discovery, celebration, and (you fill in the blank).*

*I look forward to speaking with you whenever possible. ... I sit with myself here in Sedona and hold you in my heart as best I can from a distance. Again, thank you for your poetry and sweet be-ing-ness.    Jeff*

I can still read that first email over and over and feel the same heart-opening response; a willingness to experience whatever the universe has in store for me. Here was a person with whom I sensed a deep spiritual connection—what I had always wanted in a relationship. Here was someone committed to a spiritual path towards *Truth* and awakening. I discovered later that the retreat teachers, who knew Jeff well, had hoped Jeff and I would connect. The planets, my sister, the room assignments, the matchmaking; it seemed all things had conspired to bring us together.

## ~ Chapter 2 ~

## GETTING TO KNOW YOU

*Life is the dancer*
*and you are the dance.*
—Eckhart Tolle[4]

The early days of our relationship consisted of trips back and forth between Seattle, San Francisco, Salinas, and Santa Cruz. Within a few weeks of our meeting, Jeff traveled to Seattle to visit. He arrived at baggage claim carrying a bundle of flowers that had actually survived the plane trip. I intended to show him around the city but he preferred to do nothing but sit, talk, and get to know each other.

Some of my past intimate relationships had been fraught with insecurities. At times, I felt "lost" in relationships and found myself losing touch with what was important to me. I saw that these were my own issues; they didn't come from the men in my life. Eventually, as time progressed, dissatisfactions would arise—and I would want my partner to change to accommodate my way of thinking or preferred style of living. In the early days with Jeff, I felt completely comfortable and at ease with him, and with us as a couple. I believed that neither of us needed to change to make this relationship work. It was refreshing.

During that first visit, Jeff and I would pass the time reading to each other. We read the non-dual teachings of the famous Indian sages Ramana Maharshi and Papaji. We read the poetry of Rumi and Hafiz. We read day after day, sharing heart to heart. We took walks in the neighborhood and sipped tea in the local tearoom. I hesitated to let my friends know he was in town, as I didn't want to feel obligated to introduce him to everyone. I'd shared my excitement with a few of my intimate friends and they respected my desire for this private time with Jeff.

As our time together unfolded, Jeff relayed stories about his many years being part of an ashram, which focused on non-dual, Advaita Vedanta teachings. This community of spiritual friends had been a significant part of his early life. I was somewhat envious of the wealth of spiritual support he had received from that community. Despite a traumatic break from the ashram some years before, he continued his friendships from that time. He also told me of his extensive travels in Bali and Central and South America, his brief adventures as a merchant marine and his years of diverse jobs ranging from massage therapist to housing remodeler. After much experience of life, Jeff had chosen to attend graduate school in psychology and was now a practicing counselor.

The next stretch of days I had off from work was my first opportunity to visit Jeff on his turf. Or, more accurately stated, his "turfs." Little did I imagine what was in store for me.

Jeff had several homes. One was his childhood family home in San Francisco. It had been carved up into three different living spaces and he had the top floor. Another was a single-family house located in Salinas, an agricultural valley more than two hours south of San Francisco. Lastly, there was a house in the beach town of Santa Cruz that he had rented for more than 25 years. This house had always been shared with two or more other housemates. For the first thirteen years, Jeff's housemates were connected with his ashram. He described his household after his break from the ashram as secular, but a few of the residents still shared spiritual interests. Hearing of his many years of life in communal housing was fascinating to me. Other than a time in my early twenties, I had mostly lived alone except when I was married. It was hard to imagine living for so long with so many people and so little privacy.

My first trip south was a non-stop whirlwind touching on each of Jeff's homes. The San Francisco house was full of texture, color, coziness, sensual mood, warmth, life, spirit, and love. We spent several days in San Francisco; I was a happy tourist with an amazing tour guide. Then we headed down the coast to the house in Salinas. Although it was dark by the time we arrived, a man greeted us at the doorway, smiling warmly as he said hello. He had a wild look in his eyes, but seemed kind and cheerful. Inside there were many vases of flowers and two elusive cats.

Sam, our greeter, was the first of the many colorful people in Jeff's life I would come to know. Jeff met him through a friend who had previously hired Sam for temporary work. Sam had been what most people would call "homeless," but Sam insisted that it was his choice to "camp" and live off the grid. Jeff first offered Sam a place to live in San Francisco in exchange for his helping Jeff's mother, who was quite frail at the time. After Jeff's mother died, Jeff offered Sam a room in the Salinas house in exchange for house-sitting, taking care of two cats, and yard work since Jeff was there so infrequently. I would later discover that Jeff's plan was to move out of the house in Santa Cruz and into the house in Salinas. At the time of my first visit, he was finishing a remodel of the house prior to moving. Later, he would propose sharing this Salinas house with me.

After dropping off our bags and spending some time with Sam, we headed north to Santa Cruz where Jeff was scheduled to lead a therapy group with his "guys." This was a work night for Jeff in his livelihood of counseling. "The guys" was how Jeff referred to the men in court-ordered groups whom he counseled about substance abuse and anger management. Jeff counseled men who were in jail and men who were ordered to have counseling as a condition for staying out of jail. The men were from diverse cultural backgrounds. Many of them managed to stay out of jail while they were engaged in Jeff's counseling sessions, but found themselves behind bars again within months after the sessions ended.

While Jeff conducted the therapy session, I explored downtown and wandered into the *Bookshop Santa Cruz*. It was the first of what would be many visits to this bookstore while filling the evenings during Jeff's sessions. My favorite spot was at the end of the Spiritual Book aisle in an overstuffed armchair, where I passed my time reading.

Late that evening we returned to the house in Salinas. I would be introduced to the shared house in Santa Cruz on my next visit.

With few exceptions, twice a month for eight months we traveled up and down the west coast to visit each other, with each visit lasting six or seven days. In between the visits, we spent hours every night on the telephone. I felt like a love-struck teenager. Something inside me had definitely reawakened after a long sleep. My friends and colleagues heard nonstop about this exciting new relationship and I showed them Jeff's photo over and over again. It was a side of me most people had never seen—the gaga side!

Each visit to San Francisco was full of new adventures and meeting more of Jeff's friends. He was always surrounded by people. *How could one person have so many friends? How could one person even know so many people?* I began to understand as I spent more time with Jeff. He was easy to be around and exuded an upbeat kindness. He embraced people from all walks of life, and once he had made a friend, he had a friend forever. He had friends from his San Francisco neighborhood, his junior high and high school years, his early days of spiritual exploration in Santa Cruz, and his many points of contact on his continuing spiritual journey. He had friends whom he'd met when they were his clients in counseling groups. It was only slightly less surprising that he had so many friends given he had lived his entire life in the San Francisco Bay area. I began to see that Jeff's world was filled with a full-spectrum rainbow of humanity mostly concentrated within a 100-mile radius. By contrast, my life had been a series of moves around the country beginning at the age of four. I loved all the moves, but as a result, my friends were scattered from coast to coast and not so concentrated in one locale.

I learned about Jeff's early life and family when we stayed in the San Francisco house where he was raised. He was the last living member of his immediate family. His brother, with whom he was quite close, had died many years before of suspicious causes while living in Thailand. Jeff still felt the loss of his brother nearly twenty years later. His father had died about eight years before we met, a month after having been diagnosed with liver failure. His mother died four years after her husband. Jeff had begun to remodel the house before his mother died. It was now comprised of two single-floor apartments and a basement studio, with Jeff on the top floor.

One of Jeff's closest friends from high school, Eric, lived on the second floor with his partner Leolani. On the ground floor, a guy named Vinnie lived in the studio that was behind the garage. Vinnie had been a friend of Jeff's brother and in the past had worked on construction projects with Jeff's father.

Eric was the first of the residents to shock my sensibilities. The bedrooms in the third floor apartment had French doors that opened to a back deck. Stairs went from floor to floor down to the backyard. One of my first mornings in San Francisco, as I was dressing —and was only partially clothed—there appeared a sweetly smiling man at the back deck door holding a cup of coffee. There was no easy way to cover up so all I could do was throw some clothes on and, in my embarrassment, open the door.

This was my introduction to Eric, who had just trotted up the stairs to meet me and say good morning. He took my lack of clothing completely in stride and was unfazed. Next to arrive was Leolani, who brought her camera and wanted to take a photo. As surprising as that first morning encounter was, over time these visits from the floor below became welcome, full as they were of warmth and wonderful conversation. And little did I imagine how I would cherish the photo taken that morning on the back deck in San Francisco.

The history of the house explained some of its communal feel and the casual fluidity of movement of people between the three floors. Jeff and his brother had been the center of their social world. The house had always been open for drop-in visitors, and Jeff and his brother's third floor area had often been the location where close friends got together, often for parties.

On one of my visits, Jeff initiated a gathering of all his high school friends and I listened in amazement as they reminisced about those early days. Everything I had imagined that San Francisco might have been like in the late '60's and early '70's seemed to have been played out at Jeff's house on the third floor, while his parents read the newspapers on the second.

My trips to visit Jeff always included some schedule of travel between the houses. First we would spend time in San Francisco, then time in Salinas where he continued to be busy remodeling the house, and occasionally some time in Santa Cruz. It seemed odd that we didn't spend more time in the Santa Cruz house as it was close to his work and he had considered it his primary home for more than 25 years.

It seemed we were always in motion. When traveling north or south, we always took the coastal road. Route 1 along the coast of California is one of the most beautiful public byways in the country. The road between Santa Cruz and Big Sur meandered over hills, next to steep cliffs, and near the water's edge. The views around every bend were so lovely that I was in awe of this amazing planet.

I love to travel, but Jeff loved it even more. Everywhere we traveled, be it San Francisco, Salinas, or Santa Cruz, Jeff's friends were around us. It was rarely just the two of us. Since we were still in the early months of our relationship I wanted to spend time alone with Jeff, but at this point in time it wasn't happening, much to my frustration and chagrin.

Early on, Jeff made several visits to Seattle. He finally met a few of my friends. I finally got to be the tour guide, and I shared some of my favorite Seattle destinations, including the Rose Garden, the Japanese Garden, Gasworks Park, the Asian Art Museum, and Discovery Park. A highlight of one trip was our singing a duet together while at the Experience Music Project Museum. Although the majority of his ethnic art came as a result of his extensive travel to Central and South America and Bali, on those Seattle trips he enjoyed shopping for African masks to add to the massive collection that adorned his walls in San Francisco.

One night we shared dinner with two of my close friends. Jeff described a website he wanted to create where the website subscriber could write letters to their loved ones and friends that would only be opened after the subscriber's death. The idea behind the website was Jeff's belief that people don't always—or even often—say everything they really want to say to those they love before they die. The website would create an opportunity to "communicate from the grave."

I wondered if he was talking about himself. One of my friends asked, "Why wait until you die to say what you want to say? Why not say it now?" The conversation about "saying what you need to say" continued for some time with the recognition that sometimes people just aren't able to say how they feel in the moment.

During that same visit, Jeff posed a hypothetical question to me: "Do you think you could stay with someone who became very ill? Could you love him? Would you stay or would you go?"

I responded that if I loved someone there would be no question about it. I would stay. I asked him what he would do in the same situation.

He sat quietly for a few moments, then said, "I don't think I could handle it. I would leave."

This conversation was seven months before his diagnosis. Although one never knows what one will do until or unless they are faced with a situation, when the time came, I stayed. There's no knowing what would have been true for Jeff had I become ill.

Jeff's trips to visit me in Seattle were short-lived. Soon I was doing all the flying. We had already started talking about living together and had agreed that we would make our life in California, in the Bay Area, likely in the Salinas house that he was completing. He said it didn't make sense for him to spend time in Seattle because he wouldn't be moving there. From his point of view, I needed to become familiar with what was going to be my new home. Although I could see his argument, and it had a certain practical ring to it, his decision to stop visiting Seattle triggered my old insecurities. *Why isn't he interested in spending time with my friends and meeting my work colleagues? Why isn't he interested in seeing more of where I live—and have lived—for 29 years? Is my life up to now not important to him?*

I was able to question these thoughts and set them aside as nothing more than my old self-doubt and insecurities arising. These old tapes simply needed to play themselves out. Jeff was moving forward and he wanted me to move forward with him. I let it go. My spiritual path provided me with an approach to working with my discomfort. I was committed to the relationship and wanted to meet my own conditioning, reactions, and expectations with a willingness to take a more expansive view.

Early on there was curiosity and joy in meeting Jeff's friends and getting to know his world. As time progressed, I began to see the eclectic complexity of his life. The number of diverse people from all walks of life who made up his world was rivaled only by his collections of Balinese furniture and deity statues, African masks, Asian tansu chests, and Indonesian, African, and Central American tapestries. Jeff's conversations were stimulating for all involved and he could easily focus on spiritual teachers or housing remodels, poetry or politics, music or social justice, relationships or crop circles, eastern philosophy or acupuncture and herbalists—there was no end to his interests.

In the beginning, being with Jeff was easy and beautiful and magical in every way. It was like meeting my soul mate in the pages of a well-written romance novel. But to be in relationship with Jeff was to be in relationship with a village. It wasn't one on one; I was constantly sharing him and having to sort out how to relate to the others in his life. In addition to his housemates, friends, and clients there were the strangers he would engage so easily while walking down the street. He had the gift of gab. His cell phone was often engaged. He loved to talk and had a knack for drawing deep conversation out of people. He seemed truly interested in each person's experience of life, so everyone felt special when in his presence and when he or she had his ear. Jeff had love affairs of the heart and soul with each one of his friends.

I began to ask myself—and Jeff—how we would be able to truly know each other when we were continually with other people. The question often arose. I discovered much later that several of his closest friends had similar concerns; they were rarely alone with him either. It was just the nature of being in relationship with Jeff that people sought alone time with him.

It was our shared spiritual journey that tempered my concern about the lack of time alone with Jeff. The most important thing for both of us continued to be our desire for *Truth*, for awakening to *Truth*. For me, this journey of awakening began as an investigation into the nature of experience and how the world is perceived. My initial curiosity led me to ponder the questions "Who am I?" and "What am I?" on a deep core level, which I sensed was leading me beyond all physical, psychological, familial and spiritual identities to see what remained. My narrow personal identification had started to dissolve and I was ready to know myself as an infinitely more spacious *be-ing-ness*.

I wanted to completely, fully understand this knowing in the depths of my being—I wanted to *grok* it. I was walking a challenging edge between my personal integrity in relationship and my release of personal agendas in my spiritual journey. Jeff and I had vowed to walk the path of awakening together, and that was our deepest bond. There were questions and doubts that would arise in our relationship, but there was always a return to this sense of spiritual journey that had brought us together.

## ~ Chapter 3 ~

## THE DIAGNOSIS

*Even within the seemingly most unacceptable and painful situation is concealed a deeper good, and within every disaster is contained the seed of grace. Acceptance of the unacceptable is the greatest source of grace in this world.*

—Eckhart Tolle[5]

Long before the diagnosis that redefined our relationship, I learned how Jeff viewed western medicine. When he opened his suitcase on his first trip to Seattle, I saw bottle after bottle of supplements and vitamins. He had been diagnosed with Type 2 diabetes a year earlier and he believed these supplements—in addition to dietary changes and exercise—had kept him off oral anti-glycemic medication.

I would later discover that taking so many supplements was a new behavior since the diagnosis of his diabetes. Before that he rarely, if ever, took supplements. He also had a much broader diet before his changes in response to the diabetes—he ate most things except meat and even enjoyed a glass of wine with meals. By the time I met him, Jeff was a complete vegetarian; he blended smoothies for breakfast, rarely drank wine and took roughly twenty supplements daily. Despite his healthy diet, all of those pills, and a habit of daily exercise, Jeff developed a respiratory tract infection that lasted for nearly three months. I found this puzzling. It isn't normal for a person with even average vitality and a healthy immune system to have such a prolonged infection.

The respiratory tract infection finally resolved. I was relieved to see that Jeff was feeling better, but he was much less energetic than prior to the illness. Shortly after my arrival on one visit to the Bay Area, Jeff started talking about a new concern. He was experiencing belly pain unlike anything he had ever experienced before. He described it to me—an intractable, but somewhat intermittent pain that affected his appetite, woke him up at night, and failed to fully respond to any of the remedies he had tried. Some over-the-counter treatments had worked for a day or two, and he had been certain that he had found the answer. But these "successes" were brief and the symptoms would arise again. The over-the-counter treatments only provided a tantalizing respite from his pain. So he would head to the health food store one more time or consult with friends to try and find something new to alleviate his symptoms.

What he didn't do was go to a doctor or a nurse practitioner for an evaluation. I was home in Seattle after the visit when I learned of his new belly pain. We continued our nightly conversations, but Jeff sounded weak and tired. He told me he felt poorly and was now losing weight. Jeff had health insurance with a major HMO, but he never used it. My suggestion that he go in for an evaluation was brushed aside. He was opposed to all western medicine and wanted to continue employing alternative measures. This stalemate went on for months and it was very confusing for me.

I had developed a profound love for this gentle soul and I hated to see him suffer. With my extensive education and experience, I knew that western medicine had much to offer. Jeff's refusal to see a doctor seemed without a reasonable basis and I wondered if he was afraid of something. I found myself imagining what life would be like without him. I felt a great emptiness and some sort of anticipatory grief. Jeff was still trying over-the-counter remedies for his belly pain, but something in me knew there was a serious problem.

I tried to get details from Jeff about his abdominal pain. Since he did not want to enter the allopathic system at this time, I thought I could identify a possible cause for his symptoms using my nursing skills and information I gleaned on the internet. I persisted in asking questions to try to pinpoint the location, timing, associations, quality, frequency, characteristics, causative factors, and any alleviating factors related to his pain. He reported a pain deep in his belly—sharp, penetrating, debilitating, intermittent belly pain that on occasion seemed to radiate to his upper mid-back. He was experiencing no diarrhea, no nausea, no vomiting, no bleeding, and no epigastric pain. My internet searches for causes of abdominal pain resulted in every possible diagnosis except pancreatic cancer. How could I have missed that?

When pain lasts as long as his had, it is never a good sign and looking for tumors is necessary. But Jeff had other ideas. Many of his friends offered possible causes for his symptoms and Jeff listened to them all. *Candida* (a fungal yeast infection) seemed to be the diagnosis *du jour*. This is a culprit cited for many symptoms commonly identified in articles on alternative health care, but I questioned whether there was any credence to these theories. But Jeff bought in to this possible explanation for his symptoms and started to explore ways to treat *Candida*.

Jeff also explored bringing more consciousness to his pain. He saw an opportunity to do self-inquiry, with questions like "Who is having this pain?" and "From where does pain emerge?" He was trying to shift away from his identification with the body and find a more spacious point of view. He also wanted to move into the pain, meet it, and hopefully move through it. I reminded him that meeting the pain, or sitting with it, or even moving through it didn't have to exclude trying to find out what was causing it, but he was still unwilling to see a doctor.

Additional factors in my inability to get him to make an appointment for medical evaluation were two patterns that developed through these months. First, it seemed his symptoms abated somewhat when I visited San Francisco, but flared each time I returned to Seattle. I wondered if he was simply being stoic during my visits. The other pattern that would play out when I was in Seattle was this: He would have an onset of severe symptoms; he would agree to call the next morning for an appointment; he would decide to try another remedy; and he would get some relief—a *Eureka!* moment—so he would not call for an appointment. In short order, the pain would return and the cycle would start again.

I continued to dig for the reason Jeff was avoiding a medical workup. My questioning finally revealed some of the underlying causes for his deep distrust of the conventional health-care system. He shared his memories of phlebotomists ignoring his needle phobia and refusing his simple request to draw blood from the large veins on the back of his hands. He told me about his open-heart surgery at the age of ten, when he became septic and nearly died. That trauma had been compounded by his mother's nervous breakdown and her admission to a mental health unit. He felt abandoned by his mother during that early time and felt he was to blame for her breakdown as he grew older. Finally, Jeff shared his lifelong intuition that he would not live past the age of 55. He was now 55.

I began to understand his fears, but still wanted him to move past them and have his symptoms evaluated. He still didn't want to see a physician and I couldn't convince him. During this period, I became increasingly frustrated with Jeff's friends who knew that this severe pain of undetermined cause was continuing, and who watched him continue with his ineffective regime of supplements. I began to think that I was the lone voice for seeking help from the knowledge base of western medicine.

What finally pushed my concern over the top was Jeff's lack of understanding in taking his vast array of non-prescription treatments. He admitted that he didn't know the contents of many of the pills. He just took them because one of his friends recommended them. He said he had not read the supplement labels to see if he was taking multiple doses of the same substance. He believed that a person could not overdose on vitamins or supplements. One day I lined up all of his bottles and read the contents of each of them to him. Numerous bottles contained the same thing, but it still didn't seem to matter to Jeff. He resisted every suggestion I made and I began to wonder if it was simply stubbornness running the show.

By this time, I was becoming weary of our struggle and found myself questioning my reactions *and* our relationship. I shared this with Jeff. His response was to liken our relationship to Yin and Yang, the complementary differences that balance the whole. I found myself softening. A part of me realized more deeply that it was his life, his pain, and his right to determine the next course of action that he felt was right for him.

This was a profound decision point for me. I could stay or I could go, but if I stayed I had to accept his personal choices. And I decided to stay. We had our differences, but the core of what we had was richer than I could ever have imagined.

My concerns about Jeff caused me to postpone my own need for medical treatment. Long before Jeff started having belly pain, I had developed hoarseness. The hoarseness worsened and my voice all but disappeared. I could only muster a strained whisper. When I initially sought evaluation, I learned that the hoarseness was due to a nodule on one of my vocal cords. I had spent many years singing and chanting, and in my job I talked all day with patients and families. It all added up to vocal strain that had resulted in a nodule. I was trying to resolve the situation through the conservative route of voice rest and dietary changes. I stopped singing and chanting and was taking different, less interactive assignments at work, but I was too busy traveling back and forth to the Bay Area to do more than that. I had a feeling that vocal cord surgery was in my future, but I kept putting it off. First I wanted to help Jeff discover the cause of his pain.

After several months of trying multiple therapies and "cures," Jeff admitted that he was not improving. He made an appointment with his primary care physician to evaluate his pain. Labs were drawn and everything that was tested—CBC, liver function, urine—looked normal. He called and gave me the lab results over the phone. I was full of questions. *Where were the labs to check his pancreatic enzymes?* He was diabetic, wouldn't that be an obvious place to look? *Where was the fasting glucose?* His finger-stick testing for his blood sugar had been abnormal for some time. I have to confess that at this particular point in time I had the belief that the center where I worked was the *gold standard* of cancer diagnosis and treatment. Maybe it was, maybe it wasn't, but that was my frame of reference. I continued to make comparisons of Jeff's health care providers to the physicians and colleagues with whom I worked, until at one point something inside me just let go and I stopped comparing.

Jeff's physician finally agreed to obtain a CT scan. Jeff scheduled it for my next visit to town and I was looking forward to being there with him. I was finally going to be able to help him traverse the western health care maze and be his advocate. Jeff greeted me at the San Jose airport and we headed to San Francisco. After arriving in radiology, we were escorted to a back corner of the clinic to a small combination sitting area and changing room. Jeff was given the contrast media to drink. He gagged at its consistency but was a trooper and gulped down the required two glasses. Several hours later, the scans had been completed and we left with assurances we'd be called with the results.

The next day was Saturday. There had been no phone call with the results. Jeff had the all too familiar severe abdominal pain. When he asked me if I thought we should head to the Emergency Room, I knew his pain must have shifted to a new intensity and quickly said yes. We were the only ones in the ER when we arrived and we were promptly escorted to a room where we spent the next eight hours. Jeff's lengthy, convoluted history was reviewed. A request was sent for the results of the CT scan. More testing began. Jeff's glucose was extremely high. He was given insulin and intravenous fluids were started. He looked so vulnerable lying there in his hospital gown as they injected him with pain medication. I looked at Jeff and saw the face of an innocent child. He did everything asked of him.

The ER on-call physician was truly wonderful. She was kind, warm and caring, and exuded confidence. She was a skillful practitioner who knew what she was doing. Having worked many years in health care, I knew I was watching a competent physician at work. All I could think was, "What a gift to medicine she is."

When she returned with the results of Jeff's tests she spoke quietly, "You have a mass in your pancreas." The tumor marker was highly elevated, over 1100, and she had proactively booked appointments for the coming week with an oncologist, a gastroenterologist, and Jeff's primary care physician. She said more, but not much more was needed. Although she would not say it, I was certain Jeff had cancer. It all made sense now—all of the symptoms—everything. We left the ER and returned home.

We arrived back at the house and talked briefly, but Jeff quickly headed to the bedroom for a nap. The morphine was working. He slept and I was thankful for that. I went to the living room to find comfort in two things that are healing to me—nature and music. I settled into the sofa to take in all that had transpired and looked out over the rooftops to the vast Pacific Ocean. I listened to my favorite Sanskrit chant. Amidst the sadness and pain I felt for Jeff, I also felt completely present in a place of spirit and calm. I experienced beautiful vibrations of love, of life, of strength—of God. I felt gratitude for all of life and I felt the strength to keep going.

On Monday morning at 8:00 a.m. the phone rang. We had just awakened. It was Jeff's primary care physician. He spoke to Jeff as we both listened.

"You have pancreatic cancer. You have multiple metastases to the liver. There is no cure. You are not a candidate for surgery. Without chemotherapy you have about four months to live, with chemo about six."

Point blank at eight o'clock in the morning. Just like that. I was shocked by the bluntness at this early hour—actually, at any hour. *Why didn't he ask us to come in for an appointment so he could tell us in person?* I realized this doctor was just a human being like all of us, and obviously not skilled in the delivery of bad news. But even allowing for that, I was stunned by this insensitive method of delivery.

After hearing this news and hanging up the phone, there was a stopping. There was a heart-opening silence and the very heart of life cracked wide open. We held each other in the silence and love held us and everything else. Everything was love. I knew in that moment that everything in existence emerged from the core of *Love*. I held Jeff and with all my heart and soul radiated immense love and healing into every pore of his being. I prayed that all of this love would transform the cancer. Thoughts raced through my heart and mind—sadness, love, loss. There was a mix of deep love for Jeff, gratitude for our relationship, immense sadness for what he would be going through and my own sorrow about losing him and our life together. In that split second, I thought of all the patients and families I had worked with in stem cell transplant. I now had a greater knowledge of what they felt, and I sensed what Jeff and I would be going through on every level of body, mind and spirit.

A few simple words strung together had changed the trajectory of life: "You have incurable, inoperable pancreatic cancer." A new chapter had begun. Biopsy. Diagnosis. Options. Man. Woman. Birth. Death. Infinity. One's residence on this earth is ultimately reduced to the hyphen between two dates. That hyphen can hold so much and be so incredibly rich. The Lord's Prayer on the head of a pin. I was very thankful to be there with Jeff when he was given this news. There was a deep unspoken love between us. In that moment, no words were needed.

On that day we started a new journey into the unknown that would be full of discussions and decisions. Life would unfold as it would and we would meet each day with all of the awareness and presence we could muster. Together, we were forging a new path up an uncharted mountain. The only choice was one foot in front of the other.

~ Chapter 4 ~

## COMING TO TERMS WITH IT ALL

*The present moment is as it is. Always.*
*Can you let it be?*

—Eckhart Tolle[6]

I returned to Seattle to prepare for my indefinite move to the Bay Area. How to begin this new chapter of the journey? I hear a small voice in my mind, *One step at a time. Meet what arises.* I move along with a sense that somehow everything is okay; I am not arguing with the reality of what is happening. For now, I am dealing with what is rather than struggling with how things might have been different. I will work at my job for several days before my departure, and I arrange to meet with a physician colleague to get his opinion on Jeff's possible treatment options.

When I make my way to his office he puts the disk of the CT scan that I've brought with me into his computer. He has the program required to display the images and data. The images come up quite quickly and he prepares to review them with me. I am glad to be with this physician I trust as he points out the tumors. Even knowing Jeff's diagnosis, I am stunned by what I see. There are tumors in the head of his pancreas and four or five large tumors in his liver. This is a textbook image of aggressive disease and clearly surgery is out of the question. The largest tumor surrounds the mesenteric artery, which provides blood to much of the abdominal area, and critical nerve bundles. All that can be done for Jeff is treatment to decrease the tumor load, for comfort only. *Comfort only.* Two more words that delineate this new trajectory: *Comfort only.* It slowly sinks in.

Actually seeing the CT scan and hearing my colleague's words hits me hard. It's not that I didn't know this and it's not as if I hadn't read about this invasive disease over and over and over on the internet, but there is a shocking finality to seeing Jeff's actual CT scan. *All those dark spots on the pancreas and liver.* It hits like a ton of bricks. *I now know what it feels like to be hit with a ton of bricks.*

That evening in my Seattle home I read through one more of my oncology textbooks. Despite all of my reading and discussions, I still want to know more. I read the pages about pancreatic cancer and the tears begin to flow. Tears become sobs. Then more sobs and I feel like my head will explode. Other than when I left a tearful garbled message for my clinic manager from the San Jose Airport as I relayed my news, I had not yet cried. I did not cry in front of Jeff. Now the grief of this diagnosis completely sinks in and it is overwhelming. How can I bear to lose my sweetheart with whom I thought I'd share the rest of my life? Nothing seems real and yet it all is so very real. My sobbing is a great release for me. In the midst of this I am aware that there is something very comforting in all of the tears and emotional release.

The next day I'm back at work. I'm thankful to have time to talk with my team—my friends—and to say my goodbyes. I feel like the universe is supporting me as my transition from Seattle to the Bay Area comes together. I am able to obtain a leave of absence for voice rest to help resolve the nodule on my vocal cord. Oddly, I have gratitude for that nodule now. Miraculously, all of the necessary health care and employment paperwork is completed in only a few days and I am free to leave my job to be with Jeff. I have dinner with my ex-husband and his wife, who offer to water my plants, temporarily take in all of my mail and cover my bills until I know where Jeff and I will be living. We decide to settle up monthly. I am thankful that twelve years after my divorce, I can count my ex-husband and his wife as dear friends. The transition seems so smooth, with everything falling into place, and I wonder at my sense of having good fortune in the face of such difficulty.

The next day at lunch another friend tells me about his experiences with his father, who had recently died. As his father's final disease progressed, chemical changes in his brain had affected his coherence and mood in a negative way. He cautions me that, in the event that Jeff starts saying negative things to me, I should not take it personally, but rather understand that his disease is talking. He advises me that even if Jeff asks me to leave, I should stay, not go. I can only tell my friend that leaving Jeff is the last thing I would ever do. At this point I can't even compute the possibility, I feel so far from it.

Packing is the next challenge. I won't be giving up my condo yet; I'll need this refuge during my necessary return trips to Seattle. I try to focus on what to take and what to leave—knowing it is all a diversion from thinking about what lies ahead. I'm just going through the motions of packing, repacking, eating a few nuts and an apple, drinking a cup of coffee. Finally the suitcases are closed. I take in the serenity of my home. All of my homes have been important to me, so essential to the shape of my life—my sanctuaries for meditation, reading, creating music, qigong, yoga, gardening, and entertaining friends. I look around and want everything to be frozen in time. Honoring this space—this home—and the time I have lived here, I am ready to go. I feel the steady presence of my entire life and all of it is with me in this moment. Everything is held here and it is very rich.

Early the next morning I fly to San Jose. My usual window seat, where I watched the plane's progress in happy anticipation of seeing Jeff, is now an aisle seat as I sense my energy as contained and inward. Music from my iPod drifts into my ears. I don't know what to expect when I arrive. My prayer is that I will be able to move through whatever lies ahead in a mindful and fully conscious way. The airplane ride becomes bumpy as we near San Jose. Thoughts of the Sedona retreat when I met Jeff pour forth. Remembering his pick-up lines and his insistent sweetness makes me smile. Lines from Rumi join my other thoughts:

> *I, you, he, she, we*
> *in the garden of mystical lovers*
> *these are not true distinctions*
> *I, you, he, she, we*[7]

It is still early morning when the plane lands, and Jeff is there to meet me. No longer is there a sense of infinite possibility in our embrace; our love is now poignant, bittersweet, but still solid and filled with resolve as we move forward, together.

Our first destination is Santa Cruz where we will meet with a naturopath recommended by one of Jeff's friends. This man is associated with a German physician who is trying to develop a vaccine for cancer. The naturopath's first suggestion is that Jeff and I travel to Germany for this vaccine. We agree immediately that such an excursion is out of the question. It feels so odd to me to put conventional Western medicine aside and embark on a completely unknown path. I do find my reaction a bit curious, however, since I am aware that there seems to be no good option with conventional allopathic medicine. I never thought I'd be involved in making choices like these, even though I am considered more open-minded about alternative medicine than many people. I am fascinated watching this naturopath in action; he actually seems to be winging it. *Where is the documentation that backs up anything he is saying?*

*Are his eyes really shifty or is that just my own projection?* Jeff listens to every word. When the consultation concludes we talk about the recommendations. Jeff decides he wants to try everything and he buys every supplement the naturopath suggests.

Next, it's back to San Francisco where we head to a medical center for a liver biopsy. Jeff is reluctant to have the biopsy performed. Perhaps resistant is a better description. His friends have advised him not to have a biopsy, stating that putting a needle in the tumor will break part of it off and cause it to spread rapidly to the rest of his body. I have heard this caution before, but so far have seen no absolute proof. We check in and go through the usual flashing of the patient ID card and Jeff's photo ID. This procedure must be paid for in advance so we are directed to the business office. There are so many hoops to jump through in health care; I'm glad I have great familiarity with how these systems work.

After completing these preliminaries, we finally head to the Radiology Department. Once there, the radiologist who will perform the procedure greets us and advises us that it will take one to two hours. The biopsy team consists of three others and this large crew leads Jeff off to do the procedure. I head to the café to pass the time.

After only half an hour, my tea finished, I return to radiology to find Jeff already dressed and walking down the hall. My first thought, *That was the fastest liver biopsy ever*, quickly becomes, *It just didn't happen.* When scanning with the ultrasound, the radiologist couldn't get a clear view of any one of the tumors in order to obtain the biopsy. Jeff, there despite his reluctance and resistance, quickly agreed to terminate the procedure when the radiologist suggested that he return the following week when there might be a clearer visual. But Jeff was now certain he didn't want the biopsy at all.  He shared his fears and doubt with the radiologist, and she agreed with him that it was a good decision to forego the biopsy.

So, he will not have one—ever. I am disheartened. Although I know chemotherapy is not an option, I realize there is a part of me that is still holding out, hoping for some conventional course of treatment. A biopsy to confirm the nature of the tumors would be necessary to enroll in any potential clinical trial. I want Jeff to keep his options open and his failure to have the biopsy closes doors. But these are doors that don't interest Jeff.

As it turns out, it is a practical blessing the biopsy doesn't happen on *this* day. Just as we are leaving the hospital, Vinnie (the family friend who lives in the basement apartment of Jeff's San Francisco home) calls Jeff's cell phone and reports a broken hot water heater in the second floor apartment of Jeff's rental triplex in the Pacific Heights section of town. Jeff is no longer being a patient, he is now functioning as a landlord, and we drive immediately to the property to assess the situation. Once there, a plan is developed that includes removing the hot water heater and a clothes dryer and replacing both of them. This is done while

Vinnie steadily drinks down a six-pack of beer.

Jeff and Vinnie wrestle with the old hot water heater and dryer and haul them down two-plus flights of stairs, then turn around and haul the replacements back up. I watch in disbelief. Jeff has been told he has cancer, has just come from an aborted liver biopsy, is experiencing significant pain, and is now hauling appliances up and down several flights of stairs. And Vinnie, who enjoys minimal rent payments in exchange for helping Jeff with his properties, drinks beer and complains about every aspect of his day and life. Jeff just takes this in stride.

Vinnie is the most difficult of the diverse people that make up Jeff's social world. He's much more than just a downstairs tenant who provides some maintenance assistance in exchange for a break in rent. There is a complicated history between Vinnie and Jeff, and Jeff's family. Vinnie worked on construction projects with Jeff's father for many years, and had an easy relationship with Jeff's dad that Jeff may have envied. Vinnie had moved in and out of Jeff's family home for years, beginning when Jeff's parents were still alive. Most significantly, Vinnie had been a close friend of Jeff's brother Doug. Jeff's relationship with Doug was the closest in his life, and Doug had died in his late twenties while in Thailand. Vinnie had also lost a brother to an early death. Jeff and Vinnie had formed a bond through their losses. Vinnie's drinking had been a problem for years, and at times he had managed to sober up. At this point in time he was anything but sober. During the time I spend with Jeff in San Francisco, I will witness

Vinnie in numerous drunken episodes accompanied by angry ranting about the unfairness of life.

After the long day that started at the airport, moved on to the medical center, then moved on again to the rental property, we returned to the house in the Sunset District section of the city to spend the night. The next morning, the usual view of the Pacific Ocean is replaced by a fog bank over the water. It is nearly mid-July but it feels like a cool, raw December morning. I would hear Mark Twain's assessment of San Francisco weather quoted many times; he said that the coldest winter he ever spent was summer in San Francisco. I can believe it on this bone-chilling July morning.

The next several days are spent researching possible therapies for Jeff. He has already started drinking fresh raw juices daily. As Jeff describes it, he is trying a variation of the Gerson therapy. The Gerson approach is to provide "extreme" nutrition to cancer patients and others through the ingestion of raw, organic juices; this is said to cleanse toxins and reactivate the body's immune system. What Jeff is undertaking is a deviation from the Gerson therapy. Jeff is trying to drink two juices daily; the Gerson diet calls for thirteen. He also tries to take all of the supplements that the naturopath recommended. Right now he is taking twenty pills daily. It seems like a lot to me—but this is nothing compared to what will come.

As the days progress, the facts of my situation become more real to me. I am on leave from work (trying to maintain voice rest to see if the vocal cord nodule will disappear) and I have moved away from my home in Seattle. This house in San Francisco and Jeff's house in Salinas are where I will be living for the foreseeable future. It is tough to imagine the future—my medical training and the predictions of Jeff's doctor and my physician colleague all suggest that my time with Jeff will be short and difficult. Yet, I am surrounded by Jeff's friends, some of whom are sure he can beat the disease. For a few there is even a kind of new-age fundamentalism at work—only positive thoughts are allowed. To think or speak in what seems to me to be realistic terms is considered dangerous to Jeff's health. I suspect that many of his friends are in denial about the severity of his disease. I realize that all I can do is be in the moment and help Jeff research potential therapies for his cancer. I hope we will find one that he will embrace.

## ~ Chapter 5 ~

## THE TREATMENT MAZE

*A Short History of Medicine:*
*2000 BC – Here eat the root.*
*1000 AD – That root is heathen. Here say this prayer.*
*1850 AD – That prayer is superstition. Here drink*
*    this potion.*
*1940 AD – That potion is snake oil. Here swallow this pill.*
*1985 AD – That pill is ineffective. Here take this antibiotic.*
*2000 AD – That antibiotic is artificial. Here eat this root.*
          —Anonymous (Source unknown)

Jeff is hesitant to tell people of his diagnosis. He says everyone will worry, they will call him incessantly, and he will have no privacy. This seems odd coming from a man who loves people and who is almost never alone, until I realize that the disclosure of his devastating illness will change everything in his social world. Jeff has always been the leader, counselor, and mentor of his friends. Further, despite his social engagement with so many people and many close friendships, Jeff has always been reluctant to share details of his inner life. Having once described his mother as having a sense of personal privacy, decorum and "southern hospitality," Jeff seems to have a tendency towards some of these same traits. So initially, only a few of my friends and his housemates are aware that he will, by virtue of his diagnosis, be forced into a new identity.

Our research into therapy options continues. As had been decided, surgery isn't an option. The largest tumor in his pancreas, given its position wrapped around the superior mesenteric artery, cannot be surgically removed. Therefore, no surgery is appropriate. I continue to research studies using various chemotherapy agents and the best one suggests the possibility of delaying death for as long as eight months, or perhaps a year. But Jeff is adamant; he does not want to have any chemotherapy.

I agree with his decision, given what I imagine his quality of life would be with chemotherapy. I am aware of its toxic effects and side effects—the depressed immune system, infection risk, anemia, bleeding, fatigue, weakness, nausea, and vomiting. All of these effects are treatable, but with every drug taken there are more potential side effects, which must be treated with more drugs in an ever-increasing cascade of medications. I know Jeff's desire is not to have therapy that will add only a compromised month or two to his life. His goal is quality of life over quantity of time. He has already decided that he does not want to pursue chemotherapy. So Jeff will be in contact with his traditional medical providers for brief periods only for pain management, for disease status testing, and for palliative therapy.

Continuing to search for some alternative treatment, in the midst of sorting through website after website, I suddenly remember a cancer therapy option that I had heard about years before. An acquaintance's husband was diagnosed with melanoma. He was given a one percent chance of survival and less than a year to live. He discovered a physician in New York who used pancreatic enzymes along with a multitude of other things to treat a variety of cancers. I had checked out this physician's website at the time and now remembered that his focus was pancreatic cancer. My friend's husband is still alive, and even though he still has tumors, he is thriving after four years of treatment. Although it is a sample of one, this is finally something positive. I can't remember the name of the physician, so I make a series of calls to get the information. Within fifteen minutes I have the name of Dr. Nicholas Gonzalez and links to his online information.

Checking the website, something resonates. There is at least some research and documentation supporting the Gonzalez therapy. Jeff wants an alternative approach to this devastating disease and this seems a much more viable option than any other we have seen. We call the Clinic and learn that one must apply to be seen by the doctors there, and not everyone is accepted. We download the extensive application. It covers the patient's medical history, psychological health, and most importantly, the available support of family and friends. Jeff completes the required multipage narrative statements and we fax all of the pages back to the Clinic. Within a week, he receives a phone call and is given an appointment in just two weeks. A new chapter begins.

Now that there is a treatment plan in the works, Jeff begins to tell his friends about his diagnosis. Once a few people find out it seems everyone knows, and Jeff's community is stunned and shocked by the news. Jeff is one of the first in his peer group to have a catastrophic diagnosis. As he predicted, many of his friends want to help him find a cure. But Jeff is confident that he has already uncovered the best therapy option with the Gonzalez Clinic and he explains this to his friends.

Jeff doesn't have any immediate family left, but he has several cousins, some of whom he has been quite close with over the years. Initially, he refuses to tell them of his illness, even after he has decided on his treatment plan. I don't understand Jeff's decision; if I were the one with the diagnosis I'm sure I would tell my family first, as I would welcome their support and love. We discuss it, but he holds firm for a time. He finally softens and tells a few of his cousins, one of whom will be an immense help, with her unending love and support in the coming months. She will travel to stay with Jeff during a few of my trips back to Seattle. He never tells another cousin who lives only a few hours away, and I will experience her anger and anguish after Jeff dies.

As soon as word gets out about Jeff's diagnosis, the emails begin. Even though Jeff has chosen his treatment plan, everyone has well-meaning suggestions. Many emails begin, "If I were diagnosed with pancreatic cancer I would . . ." Email links to cancer treatment sites arrive non-stop. It is impossible to read them all and sort through them; I can't tell which ones are just marketing hype for expensive supplements or therapies and which might be somewhat legitimate. There are literally hundreds of emails with ideas and I am overwhelmed.

Some are ideas we have already considered:

"You must go to the Gerson Clinic. They can cure pancreatic cancer."

"You must go to Germany. There is a vaccine that might cure your cancer."

Some are ideas we will consider, and Jeff will implement:

"You need to eat a raw food diet. Raw food will cure cancer."

"You must drink only spring water out of glass bottles."

"Casein causes cancer. You must avoid all dairy products including yogurt."

"You need to be in the sun several hours every day. You must be naked. Don't use sun screen."

"Don't wear sunglasses. Sunglasses block the sun from getting to your eyes which decreases the functioning of your immune system."

"Take this pill to boost your immune system."

"Cancer grows in an acidic environment. You must alkalinize the body with an alkalinizing diet."

"Cancer thrives on cold. You need to always stay warm."

"You must do this tapping sequence. It will stimulate your immune system."

"Cancer cells live on glucose. You have to stop all forms of sugar intake—including all fruits. You are feeding the cancer if you eat any kind of sugar."

And there are the suggestions that Jeff doesn't act on, creating a subtle sense of missed opportunity despite the very reasonable decision to forego them:

"You must eat a macrobiotic diet."

"Take five of these pills, four times a day. They will help. I take 20 a day and they help me."

"You must bury crystal pyramids upside down in the corners of your yard for protection."

"You must add these oxygen drops to your water. Oxygen will kill the cancer cells."

"You should have hyperbaric chamber treatments to increase oxygen in your body. It will cure your cancer."

"Vitamin C infusions will put your cancer in remission."

Finally, there are the questions people ask attempting to uncover a cause for Jeff's disease:

"What past trauma are you hanging on to?"

"What happened when you were 12? It may have precipitated immune system changes that led to this."

"What happened 10 years ago? The cancer may have started then."

These are just some of the multitude of ideas that come our way. It is frustrating that there isn't more clinical research done on non-pharmacological therapies. Of course, drug companies fund most medical research in America and worldwide, and they have no interest in treatments they can't patent. Thus, most of these alternative options are without any scientific proof of efficacy. I am still a product of western biomedicine, so I have resistance to most of it. But regardless of my interest, there is no possible way we can check out, or try, all these things.

The old adage that a little knowledge is a dangerous thing was never clearer to me as when we read through all of the email suggestions. Some of Jeff's friends, with little knowledge of the physiology of the immune system, are suggesting therapies that make no sense to me given my 29 years in health care, many of them specializing in stem cell transplant. I am no novice when it comes to cancer diagnosis, treatment and potential cures. I am aware of the statistical outcomes for pancreatic cancer. Right now there is no complete cure out there. There are a few high-profile cases of celebrities who postpone the inevitable, but they have either rare or more treatable forms of pancreatic cancer. I know the ugliness of what the body goes through with pancreatic cancer and Jeff has an aggressive advanced form of the disease.

Listening to the degradation of western medicine is as unpleasant as listening to those in western medicine who are intolerant of alternative methods. Intolerance is intolerance no matter which end of the spectrum one is on. For me it seems to be all about finding the holistic balance. There can be a blend of allopathic, traditional, alternative, spiritual, nutritional and woo-woo modalities. In fact, that is already what makes up the world of health care in most people's lives.

As time evolves I will soften. My anger and resistance will give way to curiosity and acceptance. Curiosity and acceptance aren't what's happening now, however. I am in a contracted state. I am living out of a suitcase and feel like the proverbial stranger in a strange land.

Despite the common refrain "If I had cancer I would try this, or take that, or travel to 'X' . . ." it's my view that no one knows what they will do until they are personally faced with the diagnosis of cancer. Maybe a person will try everything under the sun, maybe not. Until the diagnosis is real, no one knows what road they will take despite their most cherished convictions.

When a person receives a terminal diagnosis, any treatment choices are ultimately their own decision. Hopefully it is an informed decision that includes researching the options, talking with people, listening to their intuition, following their values, and looking at what they hope to gain from treatment. The most important thing may not be the therapy they actually choose. What is most important might be that the person believes in it. Whether it is chemo, or stem cell transplant, or oxygen drops, or eating raw food, or practicing emotional freedom tapping—what matters is that the person believes in whatever therapy he or she is undergoing. There has to be a *buy in*. None of it is easy; there is no easy road. But believing in the chosen therapy is the only way to sanely travel on this journey. And even then, in the best of cases, there are periods of doubt, questioning, anger, fear, and exhaustion.

~ Chapter 6 ~

# THE GONZALEZ PROTOCOL

*The journey of 3000 miles*
*Leads to all things*
*Raw, green and alkaline*

After wading through all of the ideas, options and opinions, we feel confident in the decision to visit the Gonzalez Clinic. This is what Jeff believes in. I start to believe in it as well. There is that one success story of a person known to me. I'm not sure that this therapy will cure Jeff, but it appears to be an option that will result in the least amount of harm to him for as long as his life extends.

We hop on a jet for New York City. Good fortune has it that my brother-in-law is working on a contract in New York and has an apartment in Brooklyn Heights. He's out of town and we are able to borrow his place during our brief stay for the Clinic intake visit. We explore the city on foot until Jeff becomes too tired. Even then our adventure continues as we take a bicycle carriage ride through Central Park near the end of the day. We meet our driver, Singh, upon whom we will depend to usher us back and forth between Manhattan and Brooklyn Heights throughout the rest of our stay.

The Clinic visits are almost anti-climactic. We spend several hours on each of two days meeting with Jeff's assigned physician who is one of Dr. Gonzalez' colleagues. There has already been a complete body metabolic screen obtained by testing a lock of Jeff's hair that we had provided. A lab in another state performs the test and provides information to the Clinic. I am a bit skeptical about this information gleaned from a few strands of hair.

On the first day, his physician takes a lengthy history and then performs a complete physical. On the second day, Jeff is offered the physician's view of his case and his personalized treatment protocol. All of the meetings are recorded. Many questions are asked and answered.

Jeff's specifically tailored treatment plan is contained in a twenty-page protocol and it includes supplements, liver detox regimens, guidelines for an alkalinizing diet, coffee enema guidelines, and a host of adjunct therapies including skin brushing techniques, beneficial bath types and more. We decide that Jeff will start taking some of the pancreatic enzymes while we are in New York and then begin the full therapy once we return to San Francisco.

We manage to have some fun amidst the rigors of the evaluation and treatment plan visits to the Clinic. Jeff loves art, and the Metropolitan Museum is nearby. We can't resist going. It is so peaceful walking among the paintings. One of Jeff's favorite artists is Thomas

Hart Benton and we search for his work. We have no luck as we comb many different galleries within the museum. Finally, at closing time as everyone is ushered out by the staff, we look in one last corner gallery. There on the wall is Jeff's favorite Thomas Benton piece. It is a beautiful painting of haymaking titled *July Hay*. In it is a rolling field of hay being hand thrashed. Curvy, flowing trees and flowers are in the foreground. Jeff says he wants to jump into the painting and melt into it. I completely understand.

There is no reason to stay in New York City. But there is also no reason to go directly home. Jeff has almost enough frequent flyer miles for us to travel between San Francisco and New York City with a stop in Sedona on the way back, and that is our plan. I remember that first pickup line "I have enough frequent flyer miles for two to go around the world . . . want to come with me?" Never would I have imagined that we would be using those miles for a trip to New York for a clinic visit for Jeff's pancreatic cancer. But as hard as this journey has been, there has been help from the universe. The frequent flyer miles. The free stay in my brother-in-law's apartment in New York. The leave of absence for my vocal cord nodule. I am grateful for all of these things.

And I'm very grateful to be spending a week with our friends in Sedona. This is a return to the place where our relationship began.  It is a poignant visit. We stay in a wonderful home; looking out the living room window there is an unobstructed view of pinion pines, junipers, cacti and beautiful, majestic red rocks. Each morning I sit outside with my breakfast gazing at this amazing expression of nature. We go for short hikes, which is all Jeff can handle. We try to mentally and psychologically prepare for what is to come next.

After our weeklong vacation in Sedona we return to San Francisco with the twenty-page protocol in hand. We read through the therapy guidelines. The "prescription" for Jeff includes a 70% organic vegetarian diet, raw organic green juices three times daily, organic coffee enemas at least twice daily, and 255 pills daily. There are pills upon waking, pills with meals, pills at bedtime, and pills every four hours. The pills are enzymes, vitamins, minerals, trace elements, antioxidants, and animal glandular concentrates otherwise known as pancreatic enzymes. Pancreatic enzymes and magnesium are to be ingested every four hours, six times daily, on an empty stomach. These seventeen pills every four hours are the mainstay of the therapy. According to the physician, these pancreatic enzymes will alter the tumors and cause them to shrink.

The coffee enema protocol completely perplexes me. Coffee enemas were first utilized as a healing modality in the 1940's and '50's. Apparently, the therapeutic action is to stimulate the flow of bile and improve the liver's ability to remove toxins and cancerous by-products. We are told that specific enzymes are involved with detoxification and that palmitates in the coffee increase the production of these enzymes. This then increases the effectiveness of the detoxification process in the liver. In addition, the theophylline in the coffee dilates the blood vessels and increases the movement, or *dialysis*, across the colon wall. For all of my initial skepticism, these coffee enemas will turn out to be the only things that give Jeff relief.

The rest of the therapy includes three different types of liver detoxification regimens lasting one week every twenty-one days, salt and soda baths, and skin brushing. There are numerous dietary restrictions. Jeff is prescribed the alkalinizing diet one of his friends had recommended. There can be no soy, meat, poultry, or fatty fish and the only acceptable dairy product is homemade, live culture, whole milk yogurt. Off-limits are bread products, sweets and oils (except, rarely, a small amount of olive or coconut oil.) Only white fish can be eaten. Jeff can have as many as three eggs daily for protein. Other than that, the diet is 70% raw and 70% vegetarian, and everything has to be organic. Water must be either spring or reverse osmosis; no regular tap water, distilled water or any other type of filtered water—one more friend's recommendation is validated. Only stainless steel pots and pans should be used. No microwaving. It is complex beyond belief. It is no wonder that the Gonzalez Clinic only accepts patients for their protocols who have a dedicated caregiver. No one could do this without help.

We order our first round of supplements, enzymes and enema supplies. Fortunately, the warehouse is located just outside of San Francisco so we are able to drive to pick everything up rather than wait for a shipment. Our first order consists of two huge boxes. *Huge* boxes primarily filled with pills. A patient once told me that it wasn't until she received and counted all of the pills required for her stem cell transplant that the solemn awe of what she was about to undergo sunk in. I see the same reaction in Jeff.

We need to get these pills organized and decide to make up little packets of pills labeled for different times of the day. We call some of Jeff's friends and set out all of the bottles of pills in front of us, divide up a supply of little plastic bags, and begin filling the bags. Three hours later we have a thirty-day supply of bags labeled morning, breakfast, lunch, dinner, bedtime, and the packets of enzymes that Jeff will take every four hours on an empty stomach. We carefully make up a schedule of what bags to take and when. Best laid plans . . . any semblance of a schedule lasted about three days.

One of the problems with pancreatic cancer is that the entire gastrointestinal tract is affected. Complete loss of appetite is common. Eating anything is difficult and it is easy to become satiated. It becomes apparent that it is important for Jeff to eat whenever he can— whenever he feels hungry. The treatment enzymes need to be taken on an empty stomach every four hours and not within an hour before or after eating. Because of Jeff's unpredictable eating pattern it is nearly impossible to take the enzymes on schedule, or for Jeff to take the required number of daily doses. This concerns me since these enzymes are the mainstay of therapy, yet we can't do more than the best we can. The only time there is any consistency in the enzyme schedule is during the overnight hours when Jeff has to wake up for the enzymes. Our nightly routine is always the same; put out the pill packets, set the alarms for twice in the night, and try to get some sleep in between enzyme ingestion.

My days are full of making organic coffee, making juices, and trying to make palatable meals. This is the greatest challenge given the strict limitations of Jeff's diet, and because I'm not much of a cook anymore. Although I enjoyed cooking much of my life, while living alone and working long hours for the last decade my domestic culinary repertoire was reduced to grilled salmon, soup, salad, and take-out. Of my new kitchen tasks, I'm most comfortable with the juicing. Jeff can only tolerate two juices daily, so I make juices morning and evening with a combination of vegetables that taste pretty good to me—beets, carrots, kale, chard, celery, romaine, spinach, cucumber, ginger, parsley and lemon.

Many people have opinions on which juicer to use and that becomes our next decision. Is it true that only a $1500 Norwalk juicer will deliver good nutrition? Jeff owns an old Champion juicer but it is gummy and grimy from years of minimal cleaning. One of Jeff's house-mates loans us a "cleaner" Champion juicer for the San Francisco house and we buy a new juicer for the Salinas house. The new juicer is highly rated, but turns out to be labor intensive to disassemble for each cleaning. When one is juicing multiple times daily the amount of time required for disassembling and reassembling a juicer really matters. Given what I know now, I'd stick with the Champion juicer and ditch the rest.

In the early days of our courtship, Jeff seemed to love raw foods. Our favorite restaurant was the raw, organic Café Gratitude in San Francisco; we spent many evenings there lingering over a meal. But that was then and this is now, and I realize that he loved raw food when it was perhaps thirty percent of his diet. Now that his diet is so limited he is quickly sick of it. It's not that he is craving pork or beef, but he craves savory flavors. Salads are barely tolerable. Soups are good but, given that he has been told to avoid oils except a teaspoon of olive oil on rare occasions, it's tough to make appealing soups without sautéed onions or garlic. He hates anything bland and bland is a good description of what is on the list of foods he can eat.

As we move deeper into the Gonzalez Clinic treatment protocol, I realize it is just a different approach to health and healing. Although it doesn't have the long, experiential history of Chinese medicine or the Ayurvedic medicine of India, it is a current approach to healing that attempts to incorporate new findings in alternative health care. Ultimately, all we can do is go by what seems to make sense and feels right intuitively. I'm struck by how little we human beings actually know about what is happening here in our tiny corner of the vast universe. I only know that anything is possible. Even what appears impossible is somehow possible. So I simply move forward.

## ~ Chapter 7 ~

## INTERLUDE

*The thought manifests as the word;*
*The word manifests as the deed;*
*The deed manifests into habit;*
*And habits harden into character.*
*So watch the thought and its ways with care*
*And let it spring from love*
*Born out of concern for all beings.*

—The Buddha[8]

What comes next is the hardest part of the story to tell. My journal entries from the first implementation of the Gonzalez protocol through Jeff's death are filled with sadness, anger, loss and pain. They reveal all of my insecurities and conditioning and are filled with struggle and emotional contraction. There were times of joy and laughter but in those months they seemed very brief. As I put this story together, I see many journal entries that are nothing short of raw emotion, documenting internal arguments with the difficulties and sorrows of each day. It seemed all-consuming. At the time, I tried to understand and make sense of it all. On the heels of my distress and complaints, often what arose was a whispered *I am sorry* for being so caught up in my own sadness. I often felt I was light-years away from being present in the moment for Jeff, or for myself.

As I am now able to step back as the witness of it all, I feel much compassion for that *me* who tearfully wrote day after day. In retrospect, I can see there was a completeness and wisdom to the journey even when it appeared otherwise. Even in my confusion there was grace, love, *presence*. At the time I was often blind to it.

Who can say why two people become a couple? Compatible couples seem to be like puzzle pieces; they fit together in just the right spots. Over time they will work through their differences. Over time they begin to understand and accept each other's idiosyncrasies. Over time they will come to share little rituals and speak their own special language.

My time with Jeff was so short. Our dance began as a deep promise to support one another's awakening to *Truth*, no matter what that support looked like, and whether or not we stayed together forever. That was our vow to each other. It was our deeply felt and explicit commitment. We had already fallen in love. This was an extension of that, necessary for both of us before moving forward. At the time we actually spoke this commitment, Jeff was checking a finger stick for his glucose level. He suggested I do the same. Afterwards, we pressed our pricked fingers together and became blood brother and sister. Our commitment was sealed. It was our little secret. We felt like little kids in doing this, but we were both thrilled.

How quickly our lives changed after this sweet beginning. As my life as Jeff's caregiver began, the life I knew before—the one that revolved around work, gardening, exercise, walks, silent retreats, yoga, being with friends, and drinking coffee at my favorite café— was no more. Before meeting Jeff, I had been feeling restless and ready for change in my life. I was ready to exchange the clouds and rain of Seattle for a warm, sunny climate. I had no idea that the change I sought, and then embraced, would look like this. I have been forced to accept that life is a complete mystery and I have been pushed to let go of all of my ideas on how it should—or will—unfold.

I spent many years working with people diagnosed with cancer and undergoing stem cell transplant. To be eligible for treatment at the clinic where I worked, it was required that patients have a full-time caregiver, or a rotation of caregivers providing complete coverage. I spent many hours with these patients and their helpers discussing therapy, side effects, and self-care. I also spent many hours encouraging the caregivers to take care of themselves; to make sure to take time away from caregiving in order to have some private time. I encouraged them to be out in nature, to take walks, to listen to music, to exercise, to meditate, or do whatever might relax and rejuvenate them.

When I found myself on the other side of those discussions, I failed at what I had encouraged other caregivers to do. In my profession, I had always thought I had a good idea of what patients and caregivers experienced, but I learned that I really didn't have as good an idea as I thought I did. Only the actual experience of caring for Jeff until his death gave me this knowledge. And I learned how easy it is to forget about oneself—to be consumed by the situation and the illness—in the caregiving journey. Every button gets pushed, every unresolved emotional issue gets triggered, and every harsh, conditioned, knee jerk response to a situation gets new life. I thought I had started this journey from a place of awareness and awakeness, with all of my old issues resolved. But the old buttons and unresolved issues had lingered in the recesses of my mind and emerged to be seen once again. They demanded to be seen, moved through, and resolved at a deeper level. All of this was what I had to experience. My prayers that love and compassion would always be my guides, and that awareness would be ever-present, were perhaps answered, but I surely did not know it in every moment.

## ~ Chapter 8 ~

## ILLNESS, SYMPTOMS, EMOTIONS—
## SURRENDERING OVER AND OVER AGAIN

*If you realize that all things change,*
*There is nothing you will try to hold on to.*
*If you aren't afraid of dying,*
*There is nothing you can't achieve...*

—Tao te Ching[9]

The five months between our return from New York and Jeff's death were a whirlwind of movement between San Francisco and Salinas with occasional side trips to Santa Cruz. I made several trips to Seattle where I put my home on the market. It was a time of meeting many more of Jeff's universe of friends. There was usually the sense that there weren't enough hours in the day to accomplish all of the aspects of the Gonzalez therapy. In the beginning there was a willingness to meet whatever came our way.

*****

Once we have both houses set up with at least a month's supply of medications, organic coffee and functioning juicers, we launch into this new chapter of our journey. My morning routine consists of waking early to clean and cut veggies, make juice, and brew coffee, making sure to put aside some of both for me to drink. All of the appropriate medications are set out in their packets. At some point during each day, I walk to the market to buy more vegetables for juicing. I savor my time on these walks, as it is one of my only breaks from the whirlwind that life has become.

By the time my morning routine is complete, Jeff awakens. We spend some time together nurturing our shared love of spirit—reading to each other or listening to a recorded satsang by a spiritual teacher. This part of the morning is beautiful.

After that is "spa time," which is what I dub those times Jeff proceeds with his coffee enemas. For this, he disappears into the bathroom for two hours twice a day. He welcomes these morning and evening spas. After spa time he often makes phone calls. He finds tremendous comfort in his weekly phone sessions with his close friend and spiritual mentor Nirmala, the spiritual teacher at whose retreat we met, and with whom we visited on our way home from New York.

How Jeff feels throughout the day is unpredictable. Every three to four weeks a new symptom appears or there is an exacerbation of current symptoms. Each new symptom results in the loss of any semblance of a routine. There are constant adjustments. And of course, with each new symptom I hear the question in my mind, *Is this disease progression?* I discover early on that Jeff does not like to call his physician at the Gonzalez Clinic to consult about symptoms. He prefers to deal with them in whatever way he intuits to be right for him at the time. My assumption that we will carefully follow his treatment protocol is proven incorrect. Jeff will do what he chooses to do. I begin to feel that I am completely responsible and utterly alone in this journey with Jeff. This feeling will continue to grow. For now, I am simply trying to be present with the unfolding of each new day.

The first symptom that becomes more pronounced is pain. It is more intense than the pain Jeff was feeling prior to the initial diagnosis. More intense, and no longer localized in the abdomen. It can be present in any number of places. It might show up in Jeff's lower belly, in his lower back, in his mid-back, or in his entire abdomen. Initially, he will try only an occasional medication to ease the pain. Acupuncture is discussed, but Jeff decides it is not an option. He wants to meet his pain and move through it. He wants to sit with it and explore it and see if it is possible to simply have pain, but not suffering. Non-dual spiritual teachings suggest that having pain is simply having a sensation in the body. Suffering from the pain is a different matter. The suggestion is that if you meet the pain without aversion or fear, you will not experience mental suffering. So, you have pain, but not suffering. Jeff believes this teaching, knows he is more than his body, but none of his efforts or meditations seem to alleviate either the pain or the suffering he experiences from it.

The pain continues to worsen, interfering with Jeff's ability to eat or sleep. It interferes with every possible activity, but he continues to refuse more than an occasional analgesic. I am aware that pain always precipitates a stress reaction in the body and that such stress reduces the efficiency of the immune system. Jeff's immune system is already compromised. Seeing him in such pain is a torture to me. He tries to be quite stoic about it all, and yet he is obviously suffering. I know well the benefits of oxycodone, morphine and fentanyl from my years working with cancer patients. But my knowledge, experience, and desire to see Jeff's pain relieved are ignored. I feel my defensiveness rising again as I try to make him understand. I expound the benefits of pain medications and try to reason with him, but he continues to pursue other methods.

I finally realize that I am primarily concerned with my own need to see him comfortable and I let go. I see that it is not Jeff who is suffering so greatly from his pain, but me who is suffering from seeing him in pain and feeling so helpless to do anything about it. I am trying to control a situation that I cannot control. Despite my years of nursing experience, I can't ease Jeff's pain.

Jeff had tried castor oil packs, warm baths, and a heating pad to alleviate the pain. The coffee enemas were the most effective, but they offered only temporary relief. Finally, not long after my surrender and acceptance of his refusal to take pain medications, he agrees to try narcotics. His doctor prescribes oxycodone tablets and fentanyl patches. After about a week of this therapy the pain is lessened and Jeff has more energy. He has more of an appetite. He is more relaxed and he begins to laugh again. I am grateful for this, for his increased energy, and for the smile on his face. Unbeknownst to us, this respite will be short lived.

After about two weeks of experiencing some pain relief, a new symptom arises. Jeff gets hiccups. At first we joke with each other about them. But it doesn't take long to see that these hiccups are not a temporary, minor problem. They continue hour after hour. Hiccup. Hiccup. Hiccup. These hiccups can be dainty little blips or major stomach-esophageal-chest upheavals. As with pain, hiccups interfere with just about everything—sleeping, eating, drinking, talking, and breathing. Most sufferers, after having them long enough, become depressed from either the immense difficulty of doing the above, or the complete lack of the above. Jeff tries drinking water, holding his breath, breathing into a bag, eating sugar—nothing works. Then as suddenly as they begin, they stop. And then they begin again. Night and day, day and night. The search for cures is ongoing. Friends do research and offer remedies—acupressure, acupuncture, chest tapping, clavicle tapping, and back massages. Many friends try to scare those buggers away, but the startle tactic never works. What finally seems to be the magic cure is for Jeff to tip his head over and drink water from the opposite side of a cup, sort of like drinking upside down. It is a body contortion. With his head bent over, he puts the cup edge on his top teeth and pours the water over his hard palate. The trick is to swallow it before it trickles out his nose. When he succeeds, the hiccups abate for a while, sometimes for hours or overnight, sometimes for only ten minutes.

What is causing these hiccups? Several explanations are offered by Jeff's different providers. One thinks it is a side effect of the fentanyl patch. Another thinks they are caused by spasms in his diaphragm. My intuition tells me that the tumors are growing. No one wants to say it, but I feel it. We go with the easiest possible remedy and look to change his analgesic. Jeff has already been taking short-acting oxycodone for breakthrough pain so it seems reasonable to me to start long-acting oxycontin. I call his physician in San Francisco and we schedule an appointment.

I am apprehensive about the visit. My first encounter with this doctor was that early-morning phone message giving Jeff his diagnosis. My second encounter was a tense phone conversation that was held just after the diagnosis. Jeff and I were eating dinner out at Café Gratitude. My cell phone rang and it was the doctor returning my call from earlier in the day. I stepped outside to talk with him about Jeff's diagnosis and therapy. He adamantly disagreed with Jeff's decision to forego chemotherapy. Further, the physician did not share my concern about his choice of a diabetes drug and his recommendation of an over-the-counter analgesic for pain management; both of which were metabolized in Jeff's already compromised liver. I truly felt I understood Jeff's medical needs more fully than this doctor did, but I had trouble convincing him of my points and was only partially satisfied by his responses.

The memories of these interactions still sting. I try

not to be defensive as we walk through the door of this physician's office today. Here we are, finally meeting face to face, and fortunately our previous encounters seem far behind us. Our interactions are respectful and from the heart. On his office desk there is a Hindu statue depicting one of the attributes of God. Given different circumstances, the three of us probably could have had some great conversations. Before the visit is over, Jeff is placed on the medications I had hoped he would be prescribed.

Following our visit with the physician, we visit with the diabetes nurse. We are given guidelines for checking glucose levels and guidelines for giving insulin. Jeff is given short-acting insulin, long-acting insulin, sliding-scale insulin and verbal and written instructions for all of it. However, as soon as we walk out of the room he begins to express reluctance about following the guidelines. He decides to check his blood sugar just once or twice daily and only use sliding-scale insulin. He hates needles, blood, and injections. I will again talk about risks and benefits in an attempt to convince Jeff to follow the guidelines, but Jeff prefers to do this, as everything, his way. Once again I am forced to see what appears to be my own need to follow well-known and well-established guidelines.

We head back to the house in San Francisco and decide to stay there for a few weeks. I am happy about this. Every time we move from one house to the other, from San Francisco to Salinas and back again, it is a major production. I have to box up and take fifty or so supplement bottles, the enema paraphernalia, the liver detox ingredients, clothes, and food—in and out of the car and up and down the stairs. The two-hour drive has become less enjoyable. I'm always relieved when we stay in one spot for more than a week.

I feel like I've been here forever, but it's only been two months since I was last in Seattle. My voice is still a hoarse whisper and I need to return to Seattle for vocal cord surgery—I can't put it off any longer. I make my plans, schedule my surgery and book my flight. Two of Jeff's cousins offer to stay with him while I am away..

~ Chapter 9 ~

## TIME OUT FOR SURGERY

*Because of an innocent misunderstanding you think that
you are a human being in the relative world seeking
the experience of oneness, but actually you are the One
expressing itself as the experience of being a human being.*

—Adyashanti[10]

The flight to Seattle is full of sweet memories and sadness. I am reminded of the many flights back and forth when I was like a schoolgirl in love. I am flying over the same coastline, the same mountains, and the same lakes, but those days of exciting new love seem so long ago. Now my days are full of worry and sadness and hope and sometimes gratitude, but a growing sense of being completely alone in this journey.

I welcome this break afforded by my pending surgery. I am happy to see my friends and my colleagues—the people who know me, and have known me for many years. At this time, no one really knows me in California. The focus of interactions with others has been and will continue to be completely on Jeff, as is appropriate given the circumstances. Yet, it occurs to me that if I were to have an accident or drop dead while in the Bay Area, no one would know anything about me or have the foggiest idea who to contact. I decide to carry a list of emergency contacts in my wallet.

Being with my friends in Seattle is a joy. Everyone at work is kind and supportive. I laugh with them. Being in my home is a delight. I have time to reflect on the shape my life has taken. On this journey of *not knowing*, I see times when everything feels so unreal and dreamlike and appreciate the times of deep gratitude for all of it. Mostly I go through the motions and get things done that need to be done, but everything has a certain transparency—nothing feels concrete. My mind wants to figure it all out and my heart simply wants to rest. I think about death; Jeff's death, my death.

Before meeting Jeff, I had just finished reading *A Year to Live* by Stephen Levine, a book recounting his journey of consciously living as if his death was approaching. He shared how such immediacy can force one to examine priorities and deal with unfinished business so that one can have a fully vibrant relationship with life before death. While reading the book I reflected on how I would live my life if I had one year, or one day, to live. I never suspected that this reality would come so close, so soon. I knew that big changes were coming for me beyond the continued journey with Jeff and its foregone conclusion. On this stay in Seattle I will put my belongings in storage and put my condo on the market. As good as Seattle has been for me, and knowing that my time with Jeff is limited, I also know that my longer-term future is not here.  Will I stay in the Bay Area or move elsewhere? I don't know, but I don't need to know that yet.

What's real now is that I feel very scattered and ungrounded. I'm living in Seattle, San Francisco, and Salinas. I live out of a suitcase amidst Jeff's things in Jeff's houses surrounded by Jeff's friends. I feel a strong desire to find some stable footing, but that currently seems so out of reach in my physical world. I try to find grounding in my heart, a center that will always be with me as I continue the journey.

My surgery is successful and I will need to return to Seattle for a follow-up visit in a month. I am instructed to maintain silence for two weeks. I welcome this forced silence. It's finally time to drive my car back to San Francisco. It is a turning point; future travel to Seattle will no longer feel like homecoming.

The drive back to San Francisco is a complex but wonderful retreat for me. Driving over the mountains on the Oregon-California border I am overcome with both immense love and grief. I see the amazing trees and the beautiful hills. My heart opens completely as I feel at one with all that is. And then my thoughts continue: *I will never share this sight with Jeff. I will never be able to share the love of a mountain hike or the intoxicating fragrance of Cedar trees with him. We will never go on adventures together. We will never make that trip to Bali together.* Tears roll down my cheeks. There is such grief. The loss of "what might have been" overwhelms me.

I plug in and turn on my iPod, and listen to music as I travel south through California. I once heard someone say that the only proof he needed for the existence of God was music. I love music. Music has saved me many times. I have chanted the sacred refrains of *Om Mani Padme Hum* or *Om Namah Shivaya* hundreds or thousands of times. I sing to music as I drive. In happier times I would sing and dance around my living room. I find my deepest connection to *Love* at times I am listening to music. Any particular piece of music can be the portal to oneness at any time. One time it might be sacred chants that transport me, another time it might George Winston's decades old *December* CD or a recording of Vivaldi's *Four Seasons.* It could be classical guitar music or folk music or an old Celtic ballad. Any number of pieces of music can touch the deep core of existence within me. Then, for me, there is a stopping of the mind's chatter. It's the silence between the notes that illuminates the sublime. I feel vastness when certain music vibrates in the core of my being: the same vastness I feel when I am in the beauty of nature, in the mountains, at the beach, walking on the earth. I feel it as a gift throughout this trip back to San Francisco.

## ~ Chapter 10 ~

## A FEW WEEKS IN SALINAS

*Everything that you see and experience are*
*interpretations of interpretations of endless possibilities*
*appearing in awareness*

—personal dialogue with Matt Kahn[11]

Upon returning to San Francisco, I find Jeff is doing well. The deck garden shows new life as his cousins, who filled in as caretakers and more while I was away, have lovingly transformed it. They have also cleared away the debris from the old dying plants in the house. They have put together a week's worth of soup for Jeff to consume. They have helped more than they can imagine. I have returned to find things calm, clean and fresh. It's the little things that make a huge difference these days.

Soon Jeff and I are on the way to Salinas to spend a few weeks. The huge agricultural fields that line the road coming into Salinas are full of salad makings. At the house, the flowers in the backyard are in full bloom. Jasmine fragrance permeates the air. The plum tree is heavy with fruit. The loquat tree has dropped fruit all over the patio. A hummingbird collects nectar from the trumpet flowers and butterflies are flitting around. These wonderful gifts from nature bring smiles of joy to my being and I am glad to be in Salinas. This yard is precious to me, and I hope I won't forget its healing presence in the coming days and weeks.

While in Salinas a birthday party is planned for Jeff and all of his friends who have August birthdays. I look forward to spending time with some of Jeff's friends in a relaxed atmosphere; perhaps I will have a chance to get to know them a bit more, and they will have a chance to truly know me.

The party is a potluck complete with barbequed fish, salads, vegetables, salsa, guacamole and fruit. Cards and gifts are shared. It is a wonderful party. I am delighted to get to know Velia and Will a bit; I had met Jeff's Santa Cruz housemates on our brief stops there, but this is the first chance to actually connect. I begin to feel more comfortable, and not quite so alone, as I find my place in Jeff's wide circle of friends.

Through August and September and October, wherever we stay, San Francisco or Salinas, there are many, many visitors to see Jeff. Friends come and sit beside him or at his feet as he lounges on a couch. And Jeff talks, offering his version of satsang. He speaks openly and deeply of *Truth*, of the things in life that matter. He questions what is real. He is curious about who each of us are—ultimately at the core of our beings—and he is curious about how people relate to each other. He has a way of drawing the best out of everyone, and seems to help his friends understand their own truths.

I notice that Jeff does not speak about himself with his friends during these intense conversations. Even in the beginning of our relationship when we were free to talk about everything without the shadow of his illness, he preferred to speak about the big *Truth* instead of his own inner reality and knowings. I remember an incident before his diagnosis when we were walking on the Santa Cruz pier with Dan, one of his closest friends. The three of us were discussing something personal and Jeff's approach to the conversation was to click into a detached counseling mode, offering suggestions as to how one might expand his or her understanding in a non-personal manner. But both of us were curious as to Jeff's inner experience of the issue at hand, and we pointed out his "therapizing" and avoidance of the question. Jeff was looking over the railing at sea lions swimming near the pier. He told us he would rather jump off the pier and swim with the sea lions than continue the conversation. He never did reveal his feelings on the subject at hand.

After Jeff's death I wanted to know who Jeff was to his friends, so I asked them. Most could talk only about how they felt in his presence or how he was able to help them with some issue or realization. Few had a sense of how he felt about things, or the inner workings of his heart and mind in relationship with his world. Although, according to Jeff, I knew more about him than many of his close friends it was not often that he revealed his innermost feelings.

During these months, when Jeff's friends came by to visit, they also offered their skills, talents and knowledge to help him with his illness. They brought the gifts of healing minerals, aromatherapy, massage, art therapy, reiki sessions, bodywork and endless suggestions for dietary changes. One friend regularly came by with raw food dishes, as she had very strong feelings that such a diet would help. Jeff would try to eat her food, but eventually he was unable to make much of a dent in the contents of the containers she brought. He might try one small bite and then be unable to continue eating. At this point, he was barely able to drink one raw juice a day, much less two, and his dislike of raw food had intensified. Despite this, he was unable to ask his friend to stop bringing her raw dishes—he didn't want to hurt her feelings. I could see the southern hospitality conditioning from his mother shining through. Hence the raw food gifts continued until it was clear to Jeff's friend that Jeff had stopped eating them.

A few days before Jeff's death, this friend confessed that mid-way through Jeff's illness she held much anger towards me. She felt that I should have been able to force Jeff to drink thirteen glasses of raw juice daily and eat all of her raw food offerings. I had the chance to share a bit of what Jeff's day-to-day life had been like at the time. By the end of our conversation I was able step back and see her deep love for Jeff and her own loss. I sensed that she now realized that Jeff and I both did all that we could. We were on common ground.

Jeff happily received the offerings of his friends. Day after day, through these months from summer into fall, I saw the rallying of his community. There was an unending meeting and greeting of the many people who came to him. During this time Jeff found the energy to meet with everyone even when he was in the midst of intense pain. He never showed his pain and few of his friends realized how severe it was. He would bring forth a burst of energy for a few hours for a visit, and then exhaustion would set in. By evening, when we were alone again, he would be completely spent.

There was no energy left for us. I was painfully aware that although I was the one constant in Jeff's day-to-day life, I had the least amount of quality private time with him. I started to resent this. I started to feel insignificant and unappreciated. I started to vacillate between feeling completely solid in our relationship and wondering what I was doing here.

As the light shortened and the leaves fell, Jeff had less ability to rally for visitors. He asked me to screen his calls and no longer wanted to talk with anyone or have company before noon or after seven in the evening. His mornings were the only time he had to himself, and it was noon by the time he was up and finished with his morning routine. By seven, he had nothing left to give.

I tried to be something of a gatekeeper, as Jeff had requested, but there were a few people who demanded to be in Jeff's presence whenever it suited them. One "friend of a friend" wanted to record a series of interviews with Jeff about his thoughts on death. It was research for a screenplay she was writing. I didn't care about her project and Jeff was tired. Jeff initially said no to the interviews and I relayed that information to her. But she persisted and had her mutual friend call Jeff to ask again. Jeff answered the phone. He often had a hard time saying no, which was why he asked me to be the "screener." The following morning she showed up. Jeff was gracious; I was furious. I left and took a walk so as not to scream at her for not having respected Jeff's initial wishes and for insisting to come when she did. Once she obtained all of the desired interviews, she was never seen again.

But in the end, this was one more lesson in *not knowing.* After Jeff's death, and just prior to the memorial service in his honor, I received a 30-second video clip of one of her interviews with Jeff; he was talking about life and death. It is something very dear to me now and I have to admit, in an odd sort of way, I am glad she was persistent.

## ~ Chapter 11 ~

## MELTDOWN

*Has it ever occurred to you that it is not happening anywhere outside your head?*

—Adyashanti[12]

The trips back and forth between San Francisco and Salinas continue. Jeff has bouts with hiccups several times each day and often at night. No medications, or changes in medication, have helped. The only source of relief is for Jeff to drink water upside down, and that doesn't always work even for ten minutes any more. Jeff has no appetite and is losing weight. His body changes daily and it's becoming very hard to remember what he looked like the first time we met.

Salinas seems to be the place where I can feel most grounded. We spend a bit more time here than in San Francisco. There is a statue of Buddha sitting on a cabinet just inside the back door. Seeing this each time I walk into the house is a comfort to me and gives me strength. I share this with Jeff. One day I return from buying groceries to find that Jeff has moved the

Buddha to a different location in the house. Before Jeff became ill, he rearranged his statues and artwork with regularity. Today is the first time he has done so in months. But rather than being happy that Jeff feels well enough to redecorate, my heart sinks. *How can he do this to me?*

I am angry that Jeff has moved "my" Buddha. I want to yell at him for moving it but instead I burst into tears. *Only a horrible person would get angry with her dying lover for moving a statue.* In that moment I am acutely aware that I have been walking on eggshells for months. I have stifled my own needs and emotions. I have not been treating this relationship as if we are equals. I haven't been true to myself and I have failed to honor my own path on this journey. One of Jeff's friends arrives and I relay to her what has transpired. She mediates as the three of us sit down and talk about the whole situation. It has never been so clear to me that assuming the role of Jeff's caretaker has had, and will continue to have, wide-ranging consequences.

By this time, my perception of everything is getting very limited. I am still living out of suitcases. Both of Jeff's houses are full of things—the tapestries, masks, furniture from Bali, and the large statues. Jeff never gets rid of anything so all of the rooms, walls, and closets are full—they are packed to the gills. I have fallen out of love with all of the things that I truly loved in the beginning. I am feeling claustrophobic. There is no place for me to even hang my clothes; there is no space for me anywhere. All I want is some closet space and some hangers to hang up my clothes. This becomes my obsession—hangers and closet space. There are no hangers. No stores seem to sell them. How is that possible?

Everything is in a jumble. I am so tired. Neither of us sleeps through the night. Alarms ring every four hours for the enzymes so there are snippets of sleep at best. I am getting cranky. I don't want to be cranky, but I am. I cry easily. My world is reduced to the size of a pinpoint. I am feeling loss after loss—my home, my friends, my job, my lover, our intimacy, and any semblance of an identity that I used to have. I know I am off the charts on the scale of stress-inducing life changes.

We move between houses continually and I still don't know anyone here well enough to share and talk about these feelings. I have several friends in Seattle I speak with, but it's not easy to relay all that is happening on an ongoing basis. *You have to be here to truly understand.* This complex and difficult reality can't be condensed into a ten-minute phone call. I can't talk with Jeff about any of this. I don't want to burden him. Our one reliable ritual of listening to an online satsang together in the morning doesn't even work for me any more. It feels like everything we had is gone.

As has been the case from the beginning, and especially for the past several months, we are almost never alone. I think of the The Who's rock opera, *Tommy*, and all I want to say is *See Me*. I am aware that this is an old and familiar problem. But it's increasingly real to me now.

I wish I could look at this situation as if I am just one of Jeff's friends helping him, or that this is only a nursing job. But I can't. Here is the love of my life and I am conflicted, torn. My heart is breaking. I hate everything. There are no boundaries to protect me; there is no space I can carve out for just me. What I had with Jeff no longer exists. I have become merely the doer, the helper, the organizer, the scheduler, the human alarm clock, the juicer and more. And I'm not even doing any of these things very well any more.

I no longer meditate even though I desperately feel the lack of the silence and space it has offered me for years. I pray instead. I pray for help from God, from Divine Essence, and from my mother's spirit. I pray often, from the depth of my heart and soul. I pray to understand what is real at the core of existence. I pray for what now seems an impossible goal, for a complete awakening to *Truth*. I pray again and again and again. But my prayers don't seem to be answered. I don't feel present. I feel sad, lost, and angry, and increasingly separate from Jeff. There seems to be a huge gulf between us now. *How did we get here? How did I get here?* I need a break. I honestly don't know if I can do this anymore.

I am in our bedroom in Salinas. I hate the bedroom with its rickety ancient bed and lousy mattress. I am vacuuming with a vacuum that cost a thousand dollars around a bed that wouldn't bring twenty bucks at a yard sale. This is the bed where I try to hold Jeff at night, as he lays next me, and my shoulder aches as it encounters the rocky mattress below. I start to sob. I can't stop, even though I know Jeff is in the house and can hear me. It's hard to see through the tears, the sobs, and I push the vacuum into the corner of the bed. The bed crashes to the floor. I feel an intense sharp snap arise from the depths of my being. I am only that which cries. I am the cry and the witness of it. Everything is a blur and I am in the blur. Then I turn and catch a glimpse of myself in the bedroom mirror. I see this person crying and wonder who she is. There is no recognition; it is not me. She is completely foreign; just a body moving and the movements are crying and sobbing and now pounding on the floor. She is having a total meltdown. In a flash it seems funny to see this person with such a contorted, miserable face pounding on the floor and I almost start to laugh. Then it suddenly stops. A switch has been thrown. Everything—the wrenching sobs, the detached view of the one sobbing—everything just stops. The crumbling of my world has somehow morphed into quietude. The huge release of emotions and energy now transforms into stillness.

"You need therapy." Jeff speaks from the doorway.

I am shocked. *I need therapy?* He sees me here on the floor and stands apart, suggesting therapy? No hug? No hand offered to help me up? My awareness contracts again. But things have shifted. Nothing looks the same. Things aren't better, just different. It's another letting go; it's one more surrender. Jeff, still standing in the doorway, tells me he's sorry it's so hard. I realize therapy sounds good right now. I call a therapist whose books about relationships, love and awakening I have previously read. Not surprisingly, Jeff knows him.

It takes a few days, but a new rhythm emerges. I know there is no turning back. I am in this until the end. Jeff and I are in this together, and I will continue even though I feel so alone. The deep love is still there amidst the pain and loss. I can only return to our commitment to each other, made way back when, before the diagnosis that reset reality.

Shortly after my meltdown, one of Jeff's friends, Steve, offers to help in any way he can. Jeff met Steve around the same time he met me, and they bonded around their mutual love of ethnic music. Steve is an MD who has nearly fully recovered from a serious skiing accident that left him hospitalized for many months and he now has quite a bit of free time. His help is a great gift. He comes to stay with us for several days at a time. He helps Jeff. He buys groceries and picks up the spring water. He grinds coffee. He squeezes fresh oranges, lemons and grapefruit for the next liver cleanse. His help gives me more time.

One of the best things is that as an MD, Steve completely understands the severity of Jeff's disease and its likely outcome. I can openly and fully talk with him about this. I share my sadness and my frustrations. He understands and lets me unload. He will continue to help us in Salinas and San Francisco, whenever he is needed, throughout the remainder of this journey with Jeff. His help is a godsend.

## ~ Chapter 12 ~

## SHIFTING GEARS

*Out beyond ideas of wrongdoing and rightdoing,
there is a field. I'll meet you there...*

—Rumi[13]

In October, Jeff enters into the hospice system. One of his friends is a nurse who works with hospice and he is instrumental in getting this started. The hospice team is fabulous. The nurse who comes out for the admission interview stays and talks with both of us for several hours. It seems more like a visit with a friend. There are weekly visits with a nurse, occasional visits with a social worker, and a visit with the chaplain. Jeff is withdrawing from living *his* life, but he still talks with ease about the big picture—life, death, and the meaning of it all. He hasn't lost his mental clarity; I see it in his eyes and hear it in his speech. The hospice crew loves to come; they are enchanted by Jeff—he embraces them as he has embraced so many.

We finally make another visit to Jeff's primary care physician to discuss his intensifying symptoms, his lack of appetite, his weight loss and his ongoing pain. The long-acting morphine has provided some pain control.

The hiccups persist but Jeff is trying to live with them as best he can. His weight has dropped from 185 pounds to 120 pounds. Before his diabetes diagnosis and diet change he carried over 200 pounds on his 6'1" frame. Before the clinic visit is complete, the physician offers to write a prescription for medical marijuana.

There are studies showing that marijuana is beneficial for poor appetite and weight loss. There are studies showing that marijuana is synergistic with analgesics for pain control. California voters passed a medical marijuana law years ago, but the substance is still illegal in the Federal criminal justice system. Jeff agrees to the prescription. It is all pretty hush-hush. The physician writes a "letter of need." We are told not to lose it—there will be no copy in the chart—and to please shred the letter once the necessary license is obtained. The disparity between Federal and State laws regarding medical marijuana makes everything difficult. We are advised that we have to discover the location of a marijuana dispensary ourselves because it is against the agency's policy for the MD to give us a list of locations. We are directed to San Francisco General Hospital where Jeff will register for and obtain a license.

At San Francisco General, we locate our destination in a secluded corner of the building partially hidden by a large floor plant. The employee who enrolls Jeff into the program asks me if I want a license as well. In response to my question as to why I would need one, he explains that it is legal for caregivers to grow or possess a certain amount of marijuana—presumably for the patient who needs it. Jeff and I don't see the need for me to buy one. The license for Jeff is provided; the required payment is cash only, exact change, and no checks or credit cards accepted. Again it is all very hush-hush. Someone finally gives us a list of dispensaries in San Francisco with the caveat that you'll never know if and when a dispensary will be raided and shut down. We are told that we'll have to show Jeff's new license to gain entrance to the dispensary we choose.

Initially, Jeff wasn't sure he would actually try the marijuana, but he wanted the license just in case. Growing up in San Francisco in the sixties and seventies he smoked marijuana, experimented with LSD, and experienced spiritual insights with magic mushrooms. He'd stopped using drugs long ago after a harrowing experience in Mexico that left him out in the countryside, in the middle of nowhere, without transportation, during a driving rainstorm. He credited his good fortune of being picked up by a lone truck on a bargain he'd made with God; giving up pot was his bargaining chip. But his reluctance to try marijuana again was quickly worn down by his continuing nausea and pain. He was ready to give it a try.

There are dispensaries all over town. One can find a variety of grades of marijuana to smoke as well as any number of baked goods to eat. While driving through the Haight-Ashbury district of town, we decide to visit a dispensary there. We locate the address, park the car, and find the front door locked.  There are bars on the windows. We ring a doorbell. A guy with sunglasses and chains around his neck narrowly cracks open the door and asks for identification. I feel like saying "Guido sent us." That's how it feels. Jeff flashes his card and we both start to walk inside. The door guard steps in front of me and tells me I can't come in because I don't have a license. I am incensed and retort that we're together, and I'm coming in. As bizarre as it seems, it turns into a brief standoff before I discover that I actually do need a license to even walk in the door. The door guy finally relents and lets me in with the instructions to sit at a table facing the wall without turning around to look.

I do turn around and look. It is the ugliest space I've ever seen—stark white walls, metal cases, fluorescent lights; no art, no plants, and no smiles. It is cold and unfriendly. We learn later that there are other dispensaries in town that are clean, warm and professional. The one thing they all have in common is the possibility of being raided and closed down in an instant.

After being ushered to the table, I am given a magazine to look at while Jeff shops. The magazine is full of ads for a variety of smoking paraphernalia—vaporizers, pipes, bongs, and rolling papers—along with several fairly interesting articles. I'm fascinated by the article describing vaporization. I learn that it's the process of passing hot air through marijuana, heating the herb up enough to release its active ingredients into a vapor or steam. The marijuana is not ignited so there are no flames or smoke. As the vapors escape, the active ingredients are captured in a closed filling chamber, which has a mouthpiece on one end. Then these vapors are inhaled. Only the active ingredient, THC, is inhaled, so there is no irritation of the throat or lungs. There is no odor. It seems like a great invention and we get one for Jeff.

The marijuana helps with the nausea and Jeff eats up a storm. It's wonderful to see him eat with enthusiasm. One of his close friends experiments with different ways to use the marijuana—making a butter for use in cooking or just blending it in smoothies. Many recipes are tried and Jeff enjoys the process. Sadly, within a few weeks the marijuana becomes less effective. This isn't really surprising as it is now a certainty that the tumors are growing and impinging more greatly on his entire gastrointestinal tract. For a brief time it was a blessing to see him enjoy eating and suffer less pain.

During these months there are some particularly precious days. There are gatherings with Jeff's friends from high school. There are walks along the beach. We visit a new museum in Golden Gate Park. We meander through the park with Jeff's close friends Joe, Emmy and their daughter, Natalie. They are my favorite visitors. Emmy always brings delicious soup and salad when they make the long trek from their home further north. They are able to visit four or five times in the last months of Jeff's life and we talk together about relationships, oneness and consciousness.

One of the special times is when Eric comes up to read out loud to Jeff. From an early age, they have shared much camaraderie and many travel adventures together. There is nothing special in the content of what

Eric reads, but I sense the love that Eric shares as he tenderly reads to Jeff. It brings tears to my eyes. If I had to pick one touching and purely selfless example of an outpouring of deep love from one person to another, it would be this time of Eric reading to Jeff. It was so simple and yet so profound. How lucky to have such a friend in life.

I have believed from an early age that sound and music can be healing. Over the years, I have collected a number of ancient metal Himalayan singing bowls from Tibet. The history of how these bowls are made is quite lovely. Monks living in a few Himalayan monasteries created the bowls. The bowls are made of seven different metals that are melted together. The resulting alloy is poured over a form and as it hardens it is hammered into the shape of a bowl. During this melting and hammering process the monks chant sacred prayers into each bowl. The vibrations of the sacred chants are thereby infused into the metal of the bowl. When the bowls are played, the vibrations of the prayers are released along with the sound.

Years ago, I learned how to use the bowls for vibrational sound healing and offered sound healing relaxation sessions to a few friends. Our bodies are made up of the vibrations of particles appearing to be solid. The amount of water in a person averages roughly about sixty percent of their total body weight. Sound is vibration and these vibrations permeate water and one's body. I've now brought my bowls back to San Francisco so I can offer sound healing to Jeff. I set the bowls up for the first time and play them. Afterwards, there is a calm energy in the room and Jeff is very relaxed.

The singing bowls become part of our lives together. We both relax more and there is another turning point for us in our relationship. That openness I had experienced so briefly in my meltdown emerges again and creates a space for a new depth of love and trust. A much deeper, more unconditional love is present. There are moments of deep tenderness and there are sweet conversations, heart to heart. I feel once again the sense of connection that brought us together. The love deepens to unconditional love in the truest meaning. It is not with me all of the time, but I receive and welcome its grace.

## ~ Chapter 13 ~

## THE DECISION TO STOP

*The truth catches up with me...*
*What relief to admit this finite container*
*can never contain infinity*
*what joy to find infinity*
*needs no container*

—Nirmala[14]

One morning, Jeff awakens and as we are talking he quietly says he has made a decision. He no longer wants to take any supplements. He wants to stop all therapy. He wants to continue with the coffee enemas, although they are becoming more difficult to manage. He is ready to die. He is concerned about me and wants to know that I will be okay. There are tears. There is tender touching. There have already been many days when I've known his spirit has temporarily left his body. I can see it in his eyes; there is a vacancy. His spirit is there one minute, then gone, then back again. I tell him that I will miss him immensely. There's no knowing how life will actually unfold, but for now I am confident as I assure him that I will be okay. The energy in the house completely shifts. There is a softening, a relaxation; a stillness becomes present.

Once Jeff makes the decision to stop his therapy, we talk more about the end of life. We consider how Jeff might prepare for death on a spiritual and emotional level. We read through the *Tibetan Book of Living and Dying*. We talk about the different phases the body goes through as it finally shuts down. We talk about visualizations, prayer, and letting go. We ponder oneness and emptiness, being and becoming. We talk about how he wants to dispose of his estate. He wants to give me the house in San Francisco but I cannot accept this gift. He hopes I might continue living there after his death, keeping his things in place and renting the apartments to his current housemates. I tell him that I don't want the house because I would only sell it. For me, none of this is about money or Jeff's possessions, which I will discover is not true for a few of the others who surround him.

Thanksgiving is just around the corner. Jeff wants to try to eat a full, traditional Thanksgiving dinner. His friends from Santa Cruz want to bring the meal to us in Salinas. I am thankful for this, as my menus now consist solely of raw juices, salads, and lentil or green pea soups, which is not exactly what one wants for a Thanksgiving feast. The day is beautiful. It is a wonderful meal with delicious turkey, dressing, veggies, potatoes, and pie. Jeff eats as much as he can. There is lightness in his eyes and a bit more energy in his body.

He is warmly embraced by his friends, and he showers them with his love.

In the days after Thanksgiving, Jeff wants to talk about the process of dying. One thing that has concerned him at different stages in his illness is that there might come a time when he would lose the ability to take care of his basic personal needs. He is firm in his plan that should there come a time when he cannot care for himself he wants to be able to end his life. He wants to be in control of his activities of daily living for as long as he can be, and he doesn't ever want others taking care of him in an intimate way. He doesn't want to suffer the indignity of incontinence. He especially does not want to be unconscious with others caring for his body. He wants to be able to end his life if any of this begins to happen. He wants to have the option of suicide.

He has a frank and open discussion about this with a few of his close friends and me. One friend recommends organizations that offer information about "Death with Dignity." There is a discussion about assisted suicide and its legality. Only a few states have Death with Dignity laws; California is not one of them at this time. Another friend talks of possible methods. There is a discussion about a particular method and how this could be done so no one else would be involved. Tears well up in my eyes. There is tenderness in all of this discussion, but I am struck with a deep sense of personal loss. I realize I don't want this to happen.

I'm surprised by my reaction. In my career, I have worked with people dying from terminal illness. At some point, a patient may decide enough is enough. The patient has the right to refuse treatment. In the hospital, decisions are then made to support the patient's decision. Therapy is stopped, ventilators withdrawn, or narcotics given to ease the pain that can occur when all body organs fail. Any, or all, of this can happen when people are in the process of dying from end-stage cancer, or end-stage anything. It is a combined decision; the patient, the family, and the health care team are all involved. It is never an easy decision. In every case in my experience it felt like the most compassionate and loving course of action possible in the circumstances.

But this conversation feels different. There seems to be a great divide between what I experienced in health care and the possible suicide option Jeff seeks. I could never even kill an insect; I don't know if I could be part of this. Tears are rolling down my cheeks. This isn't how I want Jeff to die. I want to hold him in my arms and comfort him. On a spiritual level, there are questions about a suicide option. *What happens on a karmic level if Jeff chooses this path? If everything is of Divine Essence, then is his soul completely liberated no matter how he dies? Or, would it depend on what his intention was in choosing the suicide option?*

I have no answers, only questions. I tell him how I feel. Clearly, these are my issues and, should he choose this path, I will support him as best I can. His other friends offer their complete support. The entire conversation comes from a place of clarity and love in every person. There is no further talk or action about this. It seems that simply knowing that everyone supports his decision and that he has a choice allows Jeff to be more at peace.

## ~ Chapter 14 ~

## SAYING GOODBYE

*"Empty-handed I entered the world*
*Barefoot I leave it*
*My coming, my going*
*Two simple happenings*
*That got entangled"*

—Kozan Ichikyo (14th century Zen monk)[15]

It is a few weeks before Christmas, and Jeff wants to spend the holidays in San Francisco at his family home. I pack up the car and we head to the city. Jeff's disease has progressed and his condition is worsening. There is an accumulation of fluid in his abdominal cavity because of advanced liver involvement and it looks like he has a basketball in his belly. It is hard for him to take deep breaths or sleep comfortably. He also has a stent that was placed shortly after Thanksgiving for obstructive jaundice. His body is fragile and nearly skeletal. I have trouble embracing him at night. In the stillness, we lie next to each other in the only position that has been comfortable for him for the past five and a half months. He lies on his right side and I am able to put my arms around him. There is so much love and yet I realize that I am starting to withdraw from his physical form. I feel deep sadness about this. It seems to be another step in my journey of surrender and acceptance.

Jeff still manages to walk but it is nearly impossible for him to navigate stairs. He is much weaker and the fluid in his abdomen exacerbates his fatigue and makes it more difficult for him to breathe. We schedule an appointment for a palliative paracentesis, a procedure to remove some of the fluid, for comfort only. A few of Jeff's friends help him down the stairs to the car, and we all go to the medical center. The procedure goes smoothly, with the physician removing over three liters of fluid. As usual, Jeff has engaged the physician during the procedure and there is a deep exchange. There will be two of these procedures within five days, and although still weak, Jeff feels quite a bit of relief.

On the way back to the house from the medical center Jeff asks to stop at a local store to buy Christmas gifts and cards for his friends. He is determined to do this and uses a shopping cart for support as he walks around the small shop. It is both heart-wrenching and very touching to watch him. I am acutely aware that I have been a witness to the change of his body from its vibrancy to its debility.

There is much closure during this period. We sit together as Jeff dictates and I write his words for the many cards and emails to his friends. His words still flow like crystal clear water out of his mouth, without stopping, without editing, without hesitation. I am completely aware that even though his body has become weak and thin, his voice has remained unchanged. It has always been clear and strong. He sounds exactly as he did on the first day we met.

A few days before Jeff leaves his body there are traumatic moments. There is the old friend and housemate who expects Jeff to leave him the San Francisco house and is enraged that he will only receive a substantial cash bequest. Witnessing this is like watching a karmic drama unfold. Another friend wants to buy the Salinas house at a bargain price and brings paperwork, hoping Jeff will sign. By this time, Jeff is mostly unresponsive. He does not sign. Both of these incidents occur within days of Jeff dying. Both of these last acts are shocking, but I am too exhausted to do anything. I am aware that people sometimes do things in the midst of emotional loss that they might do differently under other circumstances, so I just move ahead.

We spend Christmas Eve and Christmas day with Jeff's family of friends and his closest neighbors. His body is failing rapidly now, but he enjoys the Christmas carols and the company. The brief moments when he appears to vacate his body are coming more frequently these days, and by Christmas evening he seems more gone than here. Christmas evening is spent with Eric and Leolani. After sharing a movie with them, Jeff is quite tired and we decide to go upstairs. It is clear that Jeff is no longer able to navigate the single flight of stairs. He initially refuses any assistance and tries to crawl up the stairs. After twenty minutes he finally accepts help and we are able to get him upstairs and tucked into bed.

Jeff wants to die in Salinas, but it is clear to me on Christmas night that it won't be possible for me to take him there. The day after Christmas he is semi-comatose, curled up in bed. When he manages to speak he tells me again that he does not want to die in the San Francisco house or in a hospital. He wants to be in Salinas. He loves it there.

A few weeks earlier, just as we arrived in San Francisco, the hospice social worker called from Salinas. She advised us that because we had traveled to San Francisco we were out of their service area and Jeff had been discharged from their service. In that moment, everything seemed to fall on my shoulders and I was afraid that something I might or might not do would cause him more suffering. Now, I need to get him back to Salinas so that I can honor his wishes.

After checking with local San Francisco ambulance companies, I learn they'll charge over a thousand dollars to transport Jeff but can't guarantee they will be available to take him in the morning. As a last resort I call Jeff's friend, the hospice nurse, and he gives me the name and number of a Salinas area ambulance company. Together we make arrangements for the ambulance to take Jeff back to Salinas in the morning, and because we'll be back in the hospice service area, they allow me to re-enroll him.

On what will be our last night together, I am unable to sleep in the same bed with Jeff. He is no longer *here* and I am unable to comfort him. The events of the last several days have left me completely exhausted. I haven't slept and I have to try to sleep. The San Francisco housemates offer to sit with Jeff, and his close friend Joe arrives as well. I take my pillow and blanket to the couch in the living room where Jeff always sat. I want to soak up every little bit of him that might still be here in this space. I know and dread what tomorrow will bring but now I want to escape into sleep on his couch.

When the ambulance arrives the next morning, the EMTs don't think there is enough clearance to move Jeff down the front stairs on a gurney. After looking at the rotted stairs down to the backyard, they decide to strap Jeff to a board and navigate the narrow front stairs. My car is already packed for our final move. The ambulance leaves and after saying goodbye to the neighbors, I leave. Joe drives to Salinas as well. By the time I arrive in Salinas, Jeff is already there. I am told that he woke up long enough to carry out a brief conversation with the EMT who sat with him on the ride down. Jeff's Santa Cruz housemates, Velia and Will, are at the house to meet the ambulance and get Jeff settled. They stay for several hours before leaving, and I am glad for their presence.

A hospital bed now replaces our bed, which had replaced the rickety antique. Jeff lies there and I look at him, knowing he'll be gone this time tomorrow. I will miss him deeply. It has been six months since his diagnosis. Everything happened so quickly. It has been a loving, sweet, joyful, difficult, painful, and sad journey. There has been one surrender after another to *what is*, a letting go of so much. There is still a clinging at times to *what should have been or might have been*, but in this moment I feel gratitude—for all of it.

The moment passes and I feel resistance rising up one more time. Jeff is lying in the bed and there is oozing from every orifice. His Salinas housemate Sam and his friend Joe are here and I show them how to turn Jeff, wash him, and change the sheets while he is in the bed. I have conflicting thoughts. I want Sam and Joe to leave so I can lie down beside Jeff and just hold him. But they are his friends and they want to be here too. At the same time, I don't want to do this anymore and I just want to leave. Both wanting to stay and wanting to leave are true. Both come together in a final surrender to *what is*. I let go one more time. Jeff belongs to the world, not to me.

Although unresponsive, Jeff starts to become agitated. His breathing becomes erratic. The medications I have given him aren't helping. After all these months, my mind freezes and I can't make another decision. Numbness engulfs my entire being. Somehow I am able to do one more thing, and I call the hospice service and ask for help. Everything becomes a blur. Fortunately, when the hospice nurse arrives it turns out to be Jeff's friend. I hear the sound of lovely, peaceful music and smell the fragrance of incense. I realize Sam has left the room and offered this—a final gift to Jeff.

By this time Jeff's breathing is labored and gasping. There is more oozing and it's not a pretty sight. It seems like hours, but in just minutes Jeff responds to the medications given to him. The gasping slows down and then stops, and what follows is a brief, intense spasm of his body. Then complete silence. The body releases that which has animated it for the past 56 years. Spirit makes its last exit from this body. The life force is gone. What remains is simply a shell. It is a gift to witness this transition.

Everything is completely still, except for the silent words coming from my heart. *I love you. Goodbye, my sweetie. Goodbye, Jeff. May your journey be full of love and light. Thank you for being in my life. Thank you for sharing part of your life with me. Thank you for sharing this journey with me. Thank you for being my teacher. I love you.*

I offer loving assurance to his spirit that all is well. I pick up and play one of my Himalayan bowls that is sitting nearby. As I chant my own prayer to support Jeff's spirit, I send out the prayers of this bowl's creators.

These last minutes are frozen in time and space. There is complete quiet. Everything is still. There is numbing sadness. There is deep gratitude. And there is a heart cracking wide open, once again.

# ~ Chapter 15~

## GRIEF AND LOSS

*In the morning*
*When I began to wake,*
*It happened again—*
*—You put Your lips on my forehead*
*And lit a Holy Lamp*
*Inside my heart.*

—Hafiz[16]

At one point, while going through this journey with Jeff, a friend suggested I read Ken Wilbur's book, *Grace and Grit*. It's about his journey with his wife who was diagnosed with cancer. My friend said it comforted her during the time her husband was undergoing therapy for cancer. I picked up a copy but found it too close to what I was living to want to read it. Further, I was too distracted to focus on a book. Reading requires focus and a quiet mind. My mind did not start to get quiet until several months after Jeff's death. Halfway through writing this book, it finally quieted down.

Grief is part of the human experience. It is a normal response to loss and a natural consequence of death. It is not pathologic in nature. Grief is the universe speaking through your body and emotions in a particular way.

Grief was present throughout Jeff's illness and it continued for several years afterward. I discovered an appreciation for my own process of grieving. Everyone has his or her own unique way of processing loss. There is no single way to do it, and there is no doing it wrong. It shows up how it shows up and it lasts however long it lasts.

As I mentioned in the introduction, my grieving process did not fit neatly into Kübler-Ross' stages; in fact, I couldn't make it fit at all. For me, grief needed to be felt, moved through and eventually released. You will feel what you feel, and you will eventually get through it, no matter how many books you read.

My grief was wholehearted. When the sadness arose, I grieved until I was empty, crying thimblefuls or buckets of tears. The grieving and tears could last for minutes or they could take all day. There was something in the grieving that felt very alive. In an odd way, my grief felt like a friend, a friend touching something deep inside of me. Just as quickly as the grief and tears started, they would stop, seemingly out of the blue. At times, when I noticed the stopping, there would be an awareness that it was not me who did the starting or stopping of grieving. There was no specific thought *OK, time to cry* or *OK, time to stop crying.* Without any thought at all the grieving and crying would simply start or stop.

Nothing in particular would trigger the grief or

tears. I could be standing in the checkout line at the grocery store. I might be driving towards Big Sur looking out over the Pacific Ocean or hiking in the red rocks of Sedona. I might be walking outside noticing the fragrance of the jasmine. A particular bit of writing or a poem could touch me. I might hear a beautiful song or read an old email. Anything could be a vehicle to trigger grief. Suddenly, the floodgates would open and the tears would tumble down.

As much as grieving is deeply personal, it does seem universally important to grieve; to take the time to actually feel your loss. Sometimes there would be a suggestion to help me "feel better" when someone thought it was necessary to fix the grief that caused the tears to arise. I knew there was no problem, no need for anything to be fixed. The tears didn't mean that I wasn't okay with Jeff's passing, or that I wished things were different. I just missed him. I often found in my tears the presence of love and gratitude for what we shared.

Sometimes, however, another kind of grief would arise. It was grief filled with the suffering of self-imposed distress. For me it would show up in the same way that it showed up during the most stressful times of Jeff's illness. *Did I love him enough? Why was I so upset about getting up at 3:00 a.m. to get him ice cream when he asked for it? Why wasn't I able to go with the flow more? Why was I so frustrated about all the people who wanted to come see him? Why was it such a big deal to live out of a suitcase for six months? Why couldn't I just surrender in the moment more?* These questions led to feeling that I had somehow failed Jeff, had done something wrong, or wasn't good enough. Worse yet, they seemed to signal that when the "spiritual rubber hit the road" I was a failure because I didn't move through every moment with compassion and love.

These questions were the old tapes of my conditioned thought patterns attempting to assert themselves in my awareness, one more time. My intention was to fully meet each narrow, conditioned response that arose during my journey with Jeff. That didn't always happen in the midst of the difficulties and painful emotions, but I know now that that's okay. Part of allowing *what is* is to accept that your expression in the moment is part of *what is*. This could be an aware, conscious response or it could be a conditioned response—even a rigid reaction. It is all the dance of life in the moment.

All of the deep emotions—and all of the old patterned responses that arise—are our teachers. In the spiritual journey, they are all welcome. As Rumi's poem *The Guest House* suggests:

> *...Welcome and entertain them all! Even if they're a crowd of sorrows. . . Be grateful for whoever comes, because each has been sent as a guide from beyond.*[17]

Death marks a profound rite of passage, of transition. No one really knows what happens when we die. Rituals are a symbolic way to acknowledge the fact that a loved one is no longer with us in the physical plane. There are many different types of cultural, spiritual and personal rituals that may be appropriate after the death of a loved one. Any number of group rituals can mark the end-of-life transition including funerals, wakes, cremations, memorials, celebrations, ceremonies, sitting in mourning, or chanting prayers. Jeff wanted a celebration and together with his closest friends we planned a lovely and lively memorial celebration of his life. It was as diverse as his world and included a slideshow I created with our favorite music and images of Jeff's life, as well as songs, smoothies, satsang, tears and laughter. Afterwards there was a community-style shared meal.

Personal rituals can be a way to help usher a person's spirit on to the next journey, and to reflect upon, celebrate, and feel gratitude for the person's life. Rituals can be used as a vehicle for prayer, for mourning, and for letting go. After Jeff's passing, there were a number of rituals that occurred in addition to his memorial celebration. Several friends said prayers and read from the *Tibetan Book of the Dead* for the 49 days following his death. Other friends displayed photographs, burned incense, kept vases of fresh flowers, and lit candles for a specific period of time.

In the year following Jeff's passing, I had an almost-daily ritual. Most mornings I would watch the ten-minute slide show I created for his memorial service, often shedding cleansing tears. Many of the tears were over the loss of the life we shared prior to his diagnosis when everything was so new and full of potential. Many more were about the painful, difficult times we had endured. Watching the slide show helped me process the intensity of our time together.

Spreading ashes can be undertaken as another ritual. Jeff wanted to be cremated, not buried. He had traveled extensively and saw the entire earth as his home so he requested that anyone who asked be given some of his ashes to do with whatever they desired. Hence, ashes were given away and scattered in various places around the world. Whatever form one's rituals take, they are an expression of respect for a life once lived.

*****

I have two very different photos of Jeff in my house. One depicts our time together before he became ill. When I look at it I feel our immense depth of love and connection. The other photo, taken a few months before he died, is of a near-skeletal Jeff, his face narrowed by weight loss and drawn by months of pain and discomfort. People ask why I have this photo of him. For me, it represents that very real time of sadness, confusion and questioning that was part of our journey together. The open channel of love and communication we shared before his diagnosis nearly dissolved as his illness progressed. There were periods of time when neither of us spoke to each other about our feelings—we were both just trying to get through the days. Other times were blessed with communication, humor and appreciation for each other. Although my time with Jeff began as a fairy tale, it did not end that way. My sense of the time prior to Jeff's diagnosis was that we were living life in its greatest fullness. Our shared life after Jeff's diagnosis was a life of his physical decline and the constantly narrowing scope and potential of our relationship, but this period of time became my greatest teacher.

I lost more than Jeff and our planned future together in the six months between his diagnosis and death. There were losses relating to my home, my profession, my close circle of friends, and my sense of orientation to my life and my future. Grief and confusion emerged from all of these losses. I moved in and out of love, anger, defensiveness, sadness, gratitude, frustration, compassion, joy, and surrender.

In moving through these losses and emotions, there was a natural falling away of the identities that used to make up *me*. I was no longer Jeff's lover, a nursing professional in stem cell transplant, a long-time resident of Seattle, or a member of a certain social circle. What remains now is an unexpected sense of freedom and spaciousness. Initially, the loss of all of these ways of seeing myself was disorienting. I had no idea of what was next. Most of us have been conditioned to believe that *not knowing* what's next is not a worthy trait. However, with letting go of conceptual certainty my life has become full of curiosity and possibilities, and I live with more conscious awareness.

## ~ Chapter 16 ~

## THOUGHTS FOR CAREGIVERS

*...Let the beauty we love be what we do*
*There are hundreds of ways to kneel and kiss the ground*

—Rumi[18]

Your own journey will be intense, and yet it is important to remember that those close to your dying loved one will also be going through their own processes of resistance, emotional expression, and grieving. You may find that some friends and family disappear once there is a terminal diagnosis. Jeff himself said in that early conversation with me that he didn't think he'd be able to stay close to a dying lover. This withdrawal happened with one of Jeff's closest friends. He was not able to accept Jeff's diagnosis and found it difficult to make contact. Fortunately, he made his peace with reality and reappeared a month before Jeff died. There was still time and their loving friendship was confirmed.

You may be surprised to experience family or friends coming back into your life to offer support after having been absent from your world for some time. This happened to Jeff, and he wondered why people felt motivated to come back into his life once he was diagnosed with cancer. He confided that he did not immediately trust the authenticity of these renewed relationships. Initially he questioned if they were there primarily to resolve old issues or because they wanted something from him.

As the primary caregiver, dealing with family and friends is inevitable, and as such there may be difficulties in these interactions. Early on in Jeff's illness I was viewed as an angel by a number of Jeff's friends; as time went on and Jeff's condition worsened, I occasionally became the easy target of a few friends' anger and resentment. To them, things did not evolve in the way they wanted; Jeff did not do what they wanted him to do and somehow it was my fault. I also found myself navigating through the anger and dismay of the cousin who found out about both Jeff's illness and death during the same phone call. To her I was the interloper. Fortunately, after much talking and tears she came to understand that not communicating had been Jeff's decision, and she learned more about Jeff's journey. For me, these experiences became more grist for the mill.

It helps to remember that everyone deals with illness, loss and death in different ways. Everyone is doing the best they can with whatever coping strategies they have. More than anything else in regard to this universe of friends and family, don't take things personally. Know the integrity of your intentions, honor the work you do and the love you share, and move forward.

Many things helped me move through the stress created from a multitude of causes during, and after, my journey with Jeff. I wish to share with you what I learned along the way and the strategies that helped me.

First and foremost, it's important to take care of yourself. There is a natural flow of giving and receiving in the world. If your attention is focused solely on giving, you will begin to suffer from depletion. When this happens, you will be left with nothing to give others or yourself. Give yourself permission—actually *require* yourself—to carve out time and space for whatever it is that nurtures your spirit. By doing this, your own light will shine brighter and you will have the strength to continue.

It is no secret that stress, from whatever the cause, can lead to a cascade of chemical releases in the body, which have detrimental effects on health and the immune system. Do what you can to decrease your stress level. Remember to breathe. Be aware of how stress causes a tightening in the body and check to see if you are holding your breath. Tune in during those times of tension and take some slow, deliberate, deep cleansing breaths.

Meditation is known to aid in stress reduction, but if you've never meditated before it might be difficult to get started in the middle of your caregiving journey. Give it a try, but if it seems like an effort, try something else like listening to music. You can also enjoy reading poetry or inspirational books. Make time to talk with good friends, or explore other therapeutic options if you want more structured support.

The option of writing in a journal can be calming and sustaining. Doing so will help you focus your challenges and concerns if you do seek out professional assistance. It is also a way to document daily events, for as time evolves it will be difficult to remember them, and you may want to have a record.

Exercise and physical exertion are especially good stress relievers and they give you time to be alone. Go for walks, dance or just shake out your limbs in your living room, or practice qigong or yoga. If you just can't seem to carve out much time for yourself, look for chores to do outside. Mow the lawn, tend to the garden, sweep the sidewalk or water the trees. Take the time to make yourself a healthy, nutritious meal even though it would be quicker and easier to rely on fast food. When you're able to take a break from the house, perhaps when someone takes over to give you time to go shopping, don't hurry. Another fifteen or twenty minutes away is rarely critical, and you will return in much better shape if you've slowly walked the aisles of the supermarket or the lanes of the farmer's market. Sit down and have a cup of tea in the market café.

Nature is a great healer. Take time each day to walk outside and notice the trees, flowers, birds, and warmth of the sun or the chill of the air. Simply be present and aware. You will be reminded of the deep connectivity of all of life. When things were most difficult for me, nature became my church.

It is important to accept your emotions. Allow yourself your emotions even in front of your dying loved one, family and friends. It's appropriate to let those around you know how you're feeling. Their experience of your vulnerability may help them open up to their own. One thing to note is that if you have previously experienced the death of someone close to you, any unresolved feelings from that death may arise with this one. Try to recognize and move through all of it. Tears are healing, so cry when you need to cry.

As important as it is to let yourself cry, it is also important to feel joy and allow yourself to laugh. Like tears, joy and laughter release tension and renew your spirit. So, allow yourself to feel joy or to laugh even when joy or laughter come on the heels of your bleakest tears.

When possible, incorporate a time of deep reflection and truth speaking with your loved one at the end of the day. You can use a simple tool described by Joel and Michelle Levey based on four questions that give structure to your contemplations.[19] *Where today was I inspired? Where was I surprised? Where was I stretched or challenged to grow or think in new ways? Where was I deeply moved by something that came into my life?* These questions may help you find and keep your balance day-to-day.

I'll offer a few more suggestions that may seem obvious, but as they are easily overlooked they are worthy of mention. Whenever you need help, ask for it. Even before you need help, ask for it. If you have enrolled in hospice care, make full use of the resources available to you. Get respite care for yourself. Get help with chores that need to be done, but don't need to be done by you. Listen to your body and rest when your body is tired. Get enough sleep. If you can't sleep through the night, create an opportunity for regular napping. Letting a friend or family member take over care for a few hours in the afternoon will help you keep your strength and balance, and may also help them by giving them a role in the caregiving process.

Let go of feeling that you always need to be in control. You can't possibly do everything yourself and you can't fix every problem that arises. Sometimes all you can really offer is your presence; words can get in the way. You may discover that at times to simply sit in silence with your loved one is the greatest offering you can make.

Prepare yourself for what is to come. Learn about the death process. Educate yourself so you know what to expect. It may help you feel less vulnerable and it will help you help the one you love in their dying. You also need to know what needs to happen after death. Make a list in advance of necessary logistical notifications, and make a list of loved ones, with their contact information, so you don't have to worry about leaving someone out in the confusing aftermath of death.

Lastly, get in touch with the silence within. Meditate if you can, or pray, or just take time to find gratitude and appreciation within for any part of your life; such efforts will help relax the nervous system. With that relaxation there opens a greater opportunity to rest effortlessly in that inner space of stillness and silence. Always remember to honor yourself and your own journey.

~ Chapter 17 ~

# MOVING ON

*Thus shall ye look on all of this fleeting world:*
*A star at dawn, a bubble in the stream;*
*A flash of lightning in a summer cloud,*
*A flickering lamp, a phantom and a dream.*

—Diamond Sutra[20]

In his 2005 Stanford University commencement address, Steve Jobs said, *Death...is Life's change agent.*[21] This is so true. We all share this final destination. Those who have the experience of receiving a terminal diagnosis have to face this reality and the changes it brings are infinite. Those who are caregivers for someone with a terminal diagnosis must also face this reality and the infinite changes it brings. Nothing will ever be the same. There is no going back. These platitudes are true, and how one deals with change hints at how one will deal with this kind of loss.

As I reflect on our early conversations about life, I recall the several times Jeff talked about his feeling that he would die before the age of 55. He did not expect to live to old age and he had this intuition long before he was diagnosed with cancer. How is a person's approach to life affected by such inner knowing? Such an intuition may make us mindful of each precious gift life brings, or we may just deny what we "know." In walking this path with Jeff, I could not really discern how this inner knowing affected his life. Life seemed to flow for him in a seamless way. Before and after the diagnosis, he approached and perceived life with dignity and constancy. His intuition that his life would be foreshortened did not deter him from seeking treatment and attempting to extend his life. He responded to what arose one day at a time. Jeff was as present after the diagnosis as he was before. Perhaps his lifelong intuition that his time was limited helped him move through this part of his journey with such grace.

Strangely, our brief time together felt complete to me, as if it had been an entire lifetime from our meeting as giddy teenagers to our acceptance of death as old and beloved partners in the fullness of time. Most importantly, our love and our living was deep; it felt as deep as the Grand Canyon which had been the backdrop to that first love poem I wrote for Jeff.

During the first several months after Jeff's diagnosis I often thought of an old Zen story. Although I have heard this story over the years, and have read it on several internet sites, I am unable to document its origins. Even so, I'd like to share it with you:

*Once upon a time there was an old farmer who worked his crops for many years. One day his horse ran away. Upon hearing the news, his neighbors came to visit.*

*"Such bad luck," they said sympathetically.*

*"Maybe," the farmer replied.*

*The next morning the horse returned bringing with it three wild horses.*

*"How wonderful!" the neighbors exclaimed.*

*"Maybe," replied the old man.*

*The following day his son tried to ride one of the untamed horses, was thrown off, and broke his leg. The neighbors came again to offer sympathy for his misfortune.*

*"Maybe," answered the farmer.*

*The day after, military officials came into the village to draft young men into the army. Seeing that the son's leg was broken, they passed him by.*

*The neighbors congratulated the farmer on how well things turned out.*

*"Maybe," said the farmer.*

This simple story is a reminder that each moment is exactly as it is, before our judgments about it being *good* or *bad*. Our limited knowledge makes it impossible for us to ever really know in the moment what is *good* or *bad*. All we can know for certain is that it is as it is. You will experience the full gamut of emotions in your role as caregiver. I surely did. Allow yourself to feel them and don't judge yourself for what arises. What arises may be some old habitual or conditioned pattern that is ready to be released. If you can, release it. If it's not ready to be released, just let it be. My intention was to live each day as it came without judging whether events were *good* or *bad*, staying open to how things would unfold. The stresses of the journey overwhelmed that intention. I found myself at odds with life as it was taking shape. With time and distance, I have seen how limited my view was and my judgments have lost their substance.

As much as I struggled with his delay at the time, I am now grateful that Jeff refused to see a doctor to get his abdominal pain evaluated. It gave us another four months to live and love, and to get to know each other without the knowledge of a terminal diagnosis. Learning of his illness sooner wouldn't have altered the trajectory of his disease. I spent months despairing our lack of privacy and time alone together because of the constant visits from Jeff's friends, but his large, close community turned out to be a blessing in his final days when I needed their help to navigate the loss, organize a memorial, and clear out his houses before they were sold. I see more clearly that everything in life is in service to truth; everything encountered was and is my teacher. I am grateful for the deepening of understanding that emerged from this journey; my understanding of Jeff, of myself, and of the caregiving process.

I have gratitude for the person—me—who opened as much as possible to the experience of each day, and felt the love and grace of the universe in unexpected moments as the journey unfolded. I have tremendous compassion for the person—also me—who stumbled, grumbled and resisted along the way. Now, I am simply at peace with all of it. So much that was clouded is now seen in its perfection. An ancient Buddhist teaching sums it up this way: *Out of the muddy water, the lotus blooms.* Just as a lotus grows out of the muck to produce a beautiful pristine bloom, one can be transformed by the sufferings of life. Life will go on, and it might just be beautiful, even though that's hard to imagine when you are stuck in the emotional muck.

Death may be the most powerful and mysterious of all of the events in the cycle of life. While some individuals move towards death in a manner that is characterized by negativity and fear, there is often something quite beautiful about people who know they are dying. There may be a clarity or even a radiance in their eyes. When there is no hope of a future and nothing left to be done in the face of that final "loss of control," which is death, there may be deep relaxation and a love shining through. The dying person may become much more present in their interactions with others, listening whole-heartedly and responding truthfully without the agendas and defenses that have characterized the past.

Close to the end of life, a person may simply be present in each moment, as it is, from one moment to the next. This final letting go into *what is* might be called *conscious dying.* I've seen it in my work with cancer patients; I saw it in my mother, and I saw it in Jeff. It is always beautiful to experience. For a caregiver, however, this time may be quite different. While the person dying is realizing more spaciousness and emptiness, the "now" for the caregiver can simply hold a huge amount of effort and work, and the "future" can seem like a gaping hole. It is important to recognize this and not be hard on yourself as your loved one's world seems to open and yours seems to contract.

After a loss, as one's grief subsides, there is often an experience of a new aliveness in life. There may be a realization of one's own inner strength and resilience that was not seen before, or there may be a strengthening of what was always there. Indeed, loss and grief can be a journey to one's own healing, deep understanding, and wholeness. It can be a journey to one's own heart. For me it was that and more.

The body is born and, when the time comes, the body dies. This seems obvious, but we often feel quite invincible until something shocks us into remembering that our bodies are not immortal. Take the lesson of death to heart and enjoy the gift of life, savoring each moment. Be fully present in everything you do. With the knowledge that nothing in life is permanent, make peace with change, and with death.

Through the experience of loving and supporting Jeff as he completed his life journey in the physical body, I came to a fuller understanding of the way in which a deeper unconditional *Love* underpins everything. Everything springs from this *Love* and all is of it. We are part and parcel of the *Whole* of this. Recognizing this and accepting the invitation of each moment to be more fully alive in this *Love*, while always accepting ourselves as who we are, is one of the great opportunities of this life.

# REFERENCES

1. Frydman, M., trans. (1992) *I Am That: Talks with Sri Nisargadatta Maharaj*. Durham, NC: The Acorn Press. (p. 269).

2. Kübler-Ross, E. and Kessler, D. (2007) *On Grief and Grieving*. New York: Scribner. (pp. 1-28).

3. Feng, G-F. and English, J., trans. (1989) *Tao Te Ching: Lao Tsu*. New York: Vintage Books. (p. 66).

4. Tolle, E. (2006) *A New Earth: Awakening to Your Life's Purpose*. New York: Plume. (p. 115).

5. Tolle, E. (2003) *Stillness Speaks*. Novato: New World Library and Vancouver: Namaste Publishing. (p. 71).

6. Tolle, E. (2003) *Stillness Speaks*. Novato: New World Library and Vancouver: Namaste Publishing. (p. 8).

7. Barks, C., trans. (1997) *The Illuminated Rumi*. New York: Broadway Books. (p. 60).

8. Harvey, A. (2011) *The Direct Path: Creating a Journey to the Divine through the World's Mystical Traditions*. London: Watkins Publishing. (p. 155).

9. Mitchell, S. (2006) *tao te ching: A New English Version*. New York: Harper Perennial Modern Classics. (Chapter 74).

10. Adyashanti. (2003) *My Secret is Silence: Poetry and Sayings of Adyashanti*. Los Gatos: Open Gate Publishing. (p. 1).

11. Kahn, M. and Dittmar, J.
    http://www.truedivinenature.com/

12. Adyashanti. (2003) *My Secret is Silence: Poetry and Sayings of Adyashanti.* Los Gatos: Open Gate Publishing. (p. 35).

13. Moyne, J. and Barks, C., trans. (1984).*Open Secret: Versions of Rumi.* Putney, VT: Threshold Books. (p. 8, Excerpt from Quatrain 158.).

14. Nirmala. (2008) *Living From the Heart.* Sedona: Endless Satsang Foundation. (p. 107).

15. Hoffman, Y. (1986) *Japanese Death Poems: Written by Zen Monks and Haiku Poets on the Verge of Death.* North Clarendon, VT: Tuttle Publishing. (p. 108).

16. Ladinsky, D. (2004) *I Heard God Laughing: Renderings of Hafiz.* Point Richmond, CA: Paris Printing. (p. 91).

17. Barks, C., trans. (1997) *The Essential Rumi.* Edison, NJ: Castle Books. (p. 109).

18. Moyne, J. and Barks, C., trans. (1984) *Open Secret: Versions of Rumi.* Putney, VT: Threshold Books. (p. 7, Excerpt from Quatrain 82).

19. Levey, J. and Levey, M. (1998) *Living in Balance: A Dynamic Approach for Creating Harmony and Wholeness in a Chaotic World.* Berkeley: Conari Press. (p. 223).

20.   Kornfield, J., ed. (1996) *Teachings of the Buddha*. Boston:  Shambhala Publications. (p. 141).

21.   Jobs, S. Commencement address delivered at Stanford University on June 12, 2005. Stanford University News, June 14, 2005.

## Resources for Caregivers

### Books:

Aronie, N. S. (1998) *Writing from the Heart: Tapping the Power of Your Inner Voice*. New York: Hyperion.

Bauer-Maglin, N. and Perry, D., Eds. (2009) *Final Acts: Death, Dying and Choices We Make*. Piscataway, NJ: Rutgers University Press.

Callanan, M. and Kelley, P. (1997) *Final Gifts: Understanding the Special Awareness, Needs and Communication of the Dying*. New York: Bantam.

Cameron, J. (1997) *The Artist's Way Morning Pages Journal*. New York: Tarcher.

Gaynor, M. (1999) *The Healing Power of Sound: Recovery from Life Threatening Illness using Sound, Voice and Music*. Boston: Shambhala Publications.

Halifax, J. (2009) *Being with Dying: Cultivating Compassion and Fearlessness in the Presence of Death*. Boston: Shambhala.

Kabat-Zinn, J. (1990) *Full Catastrophe Living: Using the Wisdom of Your Body and Mind to Face Stress, Pain and Illness*. New York: Bantam Dell.

Kornfield, J. (2008) *Meditation for Beginners*. Boulder: Sounds True.

Kübler-Ross, E. (1997) *On Death and Dying.* New York: Scribner.

Kübler-Ross, E. and Kessler, D. (2007) *On Grief and Grieving*. New York: Scribner.

Levey, J. and Levey, M. (1998) *Living in Balance: A Dynamic Approach for Creating Harmony & Wholeness in a Chaotic World*. Berkeley: Conari Press.

Levey, J. and Levey, M. (2003) *The Fine Arts of Relaxation, Concentration, and Meditation: Ancient Skills for Modern Minds.* Boston: Wisdom Publications.

Levine, S. (2005) *Unattended Sorrow: Recovering from Loss and Reviving the Heart*. Rodale.

Levine, S. and Levine, O. (1989) *Who Dies?: An Investigation of Concious Living and Conscious Dying.* New York: Anchor Books.

Myers, E. (1986) *When Parents Die.* New York: Penguin Books.

Nhat Hanh, T. (1976) *The Miracle of Mindfulness: A Manual on Meditation*. Boston: Beacon Press.

Rinpoche, S. (1992) *The Tibetan Book of Living and Dying.* San Francisco: Harper.

## CDs:

Adyashanti. (2006) *True Meditation.* Boulder: Sounds True.

Kabat-Zinn, J. (2002) *Guided Mindfulness Meditation.* Boulder: Sounds True.

Levine, S. and Levine, O. (1999) *The Grief Process: Meditations for Healing.* Boulder: Sounds True.

Weill, A. and Arem, K. (2004) *Self-Healing with Sound and Music.* Boulder: Sounds True.

## DVDs:

Eng, K. (2009) *Presence Through Movement: Qi Flow Yoga.* Boulder: Sounds True.

Fletcher, A. (2007) *Perfect in Ten Stretch: 10 Minute Stretch.* StratoStream Studio.

Holden, K. (2010) *Exercise to Heal: Stand Up and Stretch.* www.ExerciseToHeal.com

Holden, L. (2004) *Qi Gong for Stress.* www.ExerciseToHeal.com

# More books from River Sanctuary Publishing...

*The Siren's Guitar: A musical paddling adventure,* by Stephen Snyder, 2012. $14.95

*The Emerald Tablets for 2012 and Beyond: Ancient wisdom rewritten for the present-time truth seeker,* by Ashalyn, 2011. $19.95

*Affirmations for Everyday Living: Create more clarity, success, and joy in your life,* by Annie Elizabeth, 2010. $17.95

*The Unorthodox Life: Walking Your Own Path to the Divine,* by Kathy McCall, 2009. $15.95

*Notes to Self: Meditations on Being,* by Christy Deena, 2011. $15.95

Available from:

*www.spiritualpathfinder.com*

**River Sanctuary Publishing**
**P.O. Box 1561**
**Felton, California 95018**
*www.riversanctuarypublishing.com*

We offer custom book design and production with worldwide availability through print-on-demand. We specialize in one-on-one mentoring, with full editing and proofreading services and e-book creation available.

www.ingramcontent.com/pod-product-compliance
Lightning Source LLC
LaVergne TN
LVHW091301080426
835510LV00007B/348